OUT
OF THE
VALLEY

Other books by Betty Tapscott:

Inner Healing Through Healing of Memories

Innere Heilung (German version of *Inner Healing . . .*)

Set Free

Fruit of the Spirit

Mini-books:

Self Image

Forgiveness . . . Key to Inner Healing
(also translated into Spanish)

To: Evelyn

From: Sue / Dec. 1987

OUT
OF THE
VALLEY

by

Betty Tapscott

THOMAS NELSON PUBLISHERS
Nashville

The testimonies in this book are true and factual, but all names have been changed.

The Living Bible, Copyright © 1971 by Tyndale House Publishers, Wheaton, Ill. Used by permission. (All Scripture quotations not otherwise noted are from *The Living Bible*.)

Scripture quotations marked KJV are from the King James Version of the Bible.

Library of Congress Cataloging in Publication Data

Tapscott, Betty.
  Out of the valley.

  1. Consolation.   I. Title.
BV4905.2.T35   248.8'6   80-28343
ISBN 0-8407-2458-1

In each of our lives at different times, the Lord sends someone to walk through the valley with us.

This book is dedicated to those sensitive, compassionate, loving, obedient servants of the Lord who reach out for your hand and say, "I will walk with you."

ACKNOWLEDGMENTS

With a heart full of love and gratitude, I say thank you . . .

. . . to Shirley Stansbery for reading the manuscript for grammar and spelling. She is truly a "teacher of the year." And to Betty Jo for spending hours of proof-reading.

. . . to those who have typed on this manuscript at one time or another: Lois, Pat, Ruth. Thanks also to Sue, Marie, Ann, and Caretha.

. . . to my family who have "hung in there" with me to get this manuscript "out of the valley."

CONTENTS

I

ARE YOU
IN A VALLEY?

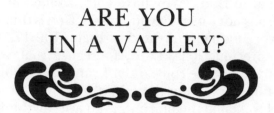

Are you in a valley right now? Is your heart breaking from grief? Has your world crumbled around you? Perhaps you're in a valley so desolate that seemingly insurmountable cliffs of disappointing circumstances rise on either side of you. Do you feel there is no hope, no escape? David felt the same way when he cried, "Oh, for wings like a dove, to fly away and rest!" (Ps. 55:6).

The Good News is that God promises He will give us a way of escape and will not send more than we can bear (see 1 Cor. 10:13 KJV). God said, ". . . whosoever shall say unto this mountain, Be thou removed, and be thou cast into the sea; and shall not doubt in his heart, but shall believe that those things which he saith shall come to pass; he shall have whatsoever he saith" (Mark 11:23 KJV).

Perhaps you are physically ill with the added burden of enormous bills mounting every day. It may be that you are standing by watching as a loved one suffers in anguish and you're wondering, "Why, God, why?"

Has the black net of depression ensnared you to the point that you feel trapped? Do you feel devastatingly alone? Do you wonder if anyone knows you are hurting—if anyone cares at all? Perhaps you've even cried out to God, "Why have you forsaken me?"

God has not forsaken you. In fact, God is thinking of you every moment of the day. Psalm 139:17,18 says, "How precious it is, Lord, to realize that you are thinking about me constantly! I can't even count how many times a day your thoughts turn towards me. And when I waken in the morning, you are still thinking of me!"

You may ask, "Well, if He is thinking of me, doesn't He know I'm still sick, that I'm depressed?" You may have sought, even frantically grasped for peace at any cost: peace through liquor, drugs, or even through the occult. But you found that none of these things brought the release of healing and freedom you so desperately needed. The answer is Jesus. "Christ himself is our way of peace . . ." (Eph. 2:14).

"But no one, absolutely *no* one has ever felt the way I feel," you say. Yes, they have. God's Word says that David cried out to the Lord, "Pity me, O Lord, for I am weak. Heal me, for my body is sick, and I am upset and disturbed. My mind is filled with apprehension and with gloom. Oh, restore me soon" (Ps. 6:2,3). In despair, he said, "Come quickly, Lord, and answer me, for my depression deepens . . ." (Ps. 143:7).

David knew that his hope and salvation rested in the Lord. God *did* take away his doubts and depression so that David shared the Good News, "The Lord lifts the fallen and those bent beneath their loads" (Ps. 145:14).

No matter what the valley, God tells us, ". . . Don't be afraid, for I have ransomed you; I have called you by name; you are mine. When you go through deep waters and great trouble, I will be with you. When you go through rivers of difficulty, you will not drown! When you walk through the fire of oppression, you will not be burned up—the flames will not consume you. For I am the Lord your God, your Savior . . ." (Is. 43:1-3).

I don't suppose there is a person alive who has not been through some kind of a valley. You may be in a valley right now. It may be a spiritual valley, but remember, ". . . greater is he that is in you, than he that is in the world" (1 John 4:4 KJV). It may be a physical valley, but the Bible says, ". . . The LORD is the strength of my life . . ." (Ps. 27:1 KJV). It may be an emotional valley: God says that "I can do all things through Christ which strengtheneth me" (Phil. 4:13 KJV).

We all have problems. Being a Christian does not mean we will be free from problems. "It is not that God loves some people more than others. Nor is it that untroubled times are evidence of His special favor. To suppose that unruffled seas and blue skies are a token of divine approval is the cruel conceit of those with whom all things go well."* First Peter 4:12,13 says: "Dear friends, don't be bewildered or surprised when you go through the fiery trials ahead, for this is no strange, unusual thing that is going to happen to you. Instead, be really glad—because these trials will make you partners with Christ in his suffering, and afterwards you will have the wonderful joy of sharing his glory in that coming day when it will be displayed."

*When You Get to the End of Yourself by W. T. Purkiser (Grand Rapids, Michigan: Baker Book House, 1970). Used by permission.

There is hope! There is a way out. We don't have to walk through the valleys alone. Jesus will walk through those valleys with us. He has sent us the Comforter, the Holy Spirit. He will send friends to help us. And praise the Lord, it is in the valley that "He restoreth our souls" (see Ps. 23:3 KJV).

We can agree with Paul, "We are pressed on every side by troubles, but not crushed and broken. We are perplexed because we don't know why things happen as they do, but we don't give up and quit. We are hunted down, but God never abandons us. We get knocked down, but we get up again and keep going" (2 Cor. 4:8,9).

Steel is soft until it is tempered by fire. Likewise, we have an opportunity to become stronger by going through trials and testings. Someone has said, "Our faith can only be measured by adversities."

Paul said, "That is why we never give up. Though our bodies are dying, our inner strength in the Lord is growing every day. These troubles and sufferings of ours are, after all, quite small and won't last very long. Yet this short time of distress will result in God's richest blessing upon us forever and ever! So we do not look at what we can see right now, the troubles all around us, but we look forward to the joys in heaven which we have not yet seen. The troubles will soon be over, but the joys to come will last forever" (2 Cor. 4:16–18).

Whatever your problem, whether it be physical, spiritual, or emotional, stand on God's promise: "For I am convinced that nothing can ever separate us from his love. Death can't, and life can't. The angels won't, and all the powers of hell itself cannot keep God's love away. Our fears for today, our worries about tomorrow, or where we are—high above the sky, or in the deepest ocean—nothing will ever be able to separate us from the love of God demonstrated by our Lord Jesus Christ when he died for us" (Rom. 8:38,39).

In the midst of the storms of life, we're to do as David: ". . . I will hide beneath the shadow of your wings until this storm is past" (Ps. 57:1).

You *can* have peace and joy, because God's Word says, "I am leaving you with a gift—peace of mind and heart! And the peace I give isn't fragile like the peace the world gives. So don't be troubled or afraid" (John 14:27).

Don't ever forget: you are loved. God loves you! You are special. He cares! Peace will come to you—it will! But it will come through Jesus, and only through Him.

Do you know Jesus as your personal Savior? Do you know Him as your Deliverer, your Healer, as your Friend who will walk through the valley with you? If you're not sure about your relationship with Jesus, if you have any doubts at all, then right now, humbly and sincerely pray this prayer:

Jesus, I know that I've sinned, and I'm sorry. I confess my sins and I ask forgiveness for them. I want You as my Savior. Please come into my heart. I love you, Jesus. It is in Your name I pray. Amen.

If you repeated this prayer with sincerity, Jesus is now in your heart, and He will not leave you. God's Word says, "If we confess our sins to him, he can be depended on to forgive us and to cleanse us from every wrong" (1 John 1:9). Romans 10:10 says, "For it is by believing in his heart that a man becomes right with God; and with his mouth he tells others of his faith, confirming his salvation."

If you have been shackled with chains of depression and despair, grief and loneliness, pain and disease, hear what God's Word in Isaiah 9:4 says, "For God will break the chains that bind his people and the whip that scourges them...." Malachi 4:2 reads, "... the Sun of Righteousness will rise with healing in his wings. And you will go free...."

Do you have painful memories that need to be healed? Jesus wants to heal those hurts. He wants to remove the "thorns" and anesthetize the wounds, to take a spiritual eraser and wipe away all the trauma of the memories.* He wants to heal those emotional wounds. He wants to fill us with His Holy Spirit. He wants to heal us: spirit, soul, and body.

God is sovereign. We must trust Him, love Him, and praise Him. Even as we're walking through our valley, it is vital that we praise Him continuously. Whether we feel like it or not, whether we want to or not, praise Him! When we wake up in the morning, all through the day, as we work, as we drive, as we sit by the hospital bed of a loved one, or as we lie in our own confining sick bed or sit in a wheelchair, as we stand behind prison doors—praise Him. You answer, "That sounds great to say just praise the Lord, but you're not in my shoes." "For now we see through a glass, darkly;

---

*A prayer for healing of memories is in Chapter 7 of *Inner Healing Through Healing of Memories,* © 1975, by Betty Tapscott. Published by Tapscott Ministries.

but then face to face: now I know in part; but then shall I know even as also I am known" (1 Cor. 13:12 KJV). Someday we will understand. But our only way out of the valley is on the wings of prayer and praise. We don't always know what God is doing or why He allows certain things to happen. Some things in life remain mysteries to us.

I want to share with you how my husband Ed and I have been touched by people who went through the very valleys I have mentioned.

Some time ago we were asked to pray for an eleven-year-old boy who had been brutally beaten and left for dead by a maniac who also murdered his grandmother. There were many tragic aspects to this case, but the light in all the darkness was the faith and testimony of the little boy and his mother. Even in pain, with his little face swollen from the beating, the youngster praised God.

That young mother, despite the grief of losing her own mother, in her dark valley of bewildering and tragic loss, continued to praise God. Her face literally glowed with the faith and love of Jesus. As the mother stayed with her son in the hospital, she and two others from her church shared the love of Jesus to the other children in the hospital ward. They used their musical gifts from the Lord to bring sunshine and joy to the patients and the nurses. The mother did not allow bitterness, hatred, or revenge to be luggage she carried through her valley.

Our lives also were touched by a Christian man when he was serving time in prison. Even in this time of darkness and loneliness, he served the Lord by working in the prison chapel and by starting a Christian library. "M" wrote joyful letters filled with hope and praise that blessed our hearts. He is out of prison now. That was his valley, but he and his precious wife can tell you: Whatever the valley, Jesus will walk through it with you.

We are all involved in a growth process which entails refining, cleansing, and a smoothing away of rough edges. Judson Cornwall, a noted teacher, speaks of life's "enlarging process." We squirm, protest, yell, when life becomes difficult—much as a new shoe creaks and resists as the shoe stretcher is expanded to stretch the leather. When the stretching is over, the shoe has become usable, pliable, and comfortable. Likewise, when we face trials, troubles, hurt, or grief, we can use that time for refining and growth. As David wrote, ". . . thou hast enlarged me when I was in distress . . ." (Ps. 4:1 KJV).

We are not to seek suffering, desire problems, or revel in pain or illness, just for the sake of being a martyr for the Lord. However, God's Word says, "When they walk through the Valley of Weeping it will become a place of springs where pools of blessing and refreshment collect after rains!" (Ps. 84:6).

Since spiritual renewal has swept across the land, we have heard and read much on the teaching of positive confession: Just confess it and you possess it; claim it and it is yours. Let me hasten to say I believe in being positive. We don't need whiny-birds or pity parties. The confetti from those pity parties pollutes the air. But. . . .

There must be a balance. Excellent books have been

written on faith versus presumption. We cannot manipulate God. He is in control. One extreme says, "Healing has ended, and God will give me the grace to bear this illness." Deliver us from that teaching! But there is the other extreme. Some are so zealous to the opposite that, even though a person is still in a wheelchair or totally blind, he or she is told to confess, "I'm healed." The skeptic looks on as the person is pushed out of the building or led from the service and he says, "Those Christians are a bunch of kooks."

There is a teaching which says Spirit-filled Christians don't get sick. And they should never, never become discouraged or depressed. If they do, a self-righteous finger just may be pointed at them accusing them of doing something wrong.

What I want to say in this book is, "Yes, God heals today and yes, He wants us to live the vibrant, joy-filled life. But, even as Christians, we may unfortunately find ourselves at times in the valley of illness. We may suffer grief or periods of discouragement, even depression. There may be times of doubt and questions, but if we balance our lives with prayer and praise, we can come out of that valley.

Our prayer is that this book will make your valley a little easier as you read how others have been led by the strong but gentle hand of Jesus. Remember, God has charted our paths, and He will go *through* every wilderness with us. God will walk *through* the valley of disease, grief, or depression by our side.

What a comfort to know that He will restore our souls in the valley. There is hope; there is help. "I will lift up mine eyes unto the hills, from whence cometh my help. My help cometh from the Lord . . ." (Ps. 121:1,2 KJV).

How glorious it is to watch people who are hurting take the strong hand of our Lord and receive strength, power, and encouragement. We can come out of the valley *victorious*! "We are more than conquerors through him that loved us" (Rom. 8:37 KJV).

II

OUT OF THE VALLEY OF DISEASE

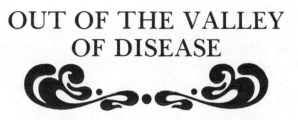

He forgives all my sins. He heals me.
—Psalm 103:3

The meeting had already started when an Indian couple carried their twenty-one-year-old daughter into the church. She could not walk and obviously was in pain. They brought her to the front where people moved over and made room for her on the second row. She laid her head against the edge of the pew and kept it there during the entire meeting. She looked so sick and weak.

After the teaching, the parents brought her to us and asked, "Would you please pray for our daughter?" We did not know the details of her problem, only that Brenda had arthritis of the spine and feet, could not walk, and was unable to stand or support her own weight.

We had the entire congregation agree with us in prayer for the Lord to heal this precious Indian girl. We bound Satan from her in the name of Jesus. We could feel the power of the Lord as we all joined in prayer.

My husband, Ed, held one of her arms; I held the other. We fervently prayed, "Oh, Lord Jesus, let her walk!" And haltingly, she took a step, then another tiny step, and then another! We all stood in awe as the power of the Lord continued to surge through her. Praise His name! Excitement and wonder raced through the church.

The parents started to cry; Brenda was crying; people all over the church were crying as they watched God display His mighty power. It was a few minutes before the mother could share with us Brenda's story. As a child, Brenda had suffered arthritis of the spine. Her feet had become crippled so that she could not walk. The doctors had told the parents there was nothing that could be done for their daughter's feet but they would attempt surgery on her spine.

In fact, the surgery had been scheduled, and she had been in the operating room of a hospital eighty miles away that very morning. The doctors had already frozen her back for the operation. The parents were sitting in the waiting room when they picked up a newspaper and read that there was to be a meeting that night where prayer would be lifted up for the sick. They became excited as they discussed it between themselves. Should they go to the meeting? Could they stop the surgery? Should they drive Brenda so far? Should they, could they, trust God to heal their daughter?

Quickly, they decided to stop the surgery. The doctors said, "If you take her out of the hospital, we will not be responsible for her. She will have to check herself out."

"That is exactly what Brenda did," the mother said.

Can you imagine the faith it took, not only on the

part of the parents, but also on the part of Brenda, to do a thing like that? God honored their faith and healed her. She walked down the stairs from the church that night completely unaided.

The next night before the meeting started, an energetic young woman passed me in the aisle. She had already gone by before I realized that it was the same girl the Lord had healed the night before!

We talked to Brenda's grandmother four months later when we were back in Canada. The grandmother said that Brenda was completely well and walking perfectly. Five months later, we received a letter from Brenda saying, "I am still healed, and I want to preach about Jesus. Pray for me, O.K.?"

Now, over a year later, Brenda is still a healthy, glowing, vibrant Christian, constantly giving God all the glory for her miraculous healing.

Thank You, Lord, for this believing family who trusted You for a miracle. Thank You for honoring that trust, Lord Jesus. You have received all the praise and all the glory.

GOD DOES HEAL TODAY!

So, the Lord healed that girl, but what about me? you say. I'm sick and I'm not sure I have enough faith to believe; or I've been sick for years, and I have the faith to move mountains, you argue. Why hasn't He healed me? These and other questions bubble to the top when the subject of healing is put on the stove. Does God heal today?

Many people believe divine healing ended when

Jesus left this earth. They believe that miracles ceased. Too many of us have prayed ourselves or heard some-one else pray, "God give me the grace to bear this illness;" rather than asking "God, please heal me," and expectantly believing that He will do so.

How many times have we been present in church when the list of hospital patients was read, and prayers were lifted in their behalf for healing. They were halfhearted prayers, with no one really expecting the sick to be healed. As one pastor said, "We pray for healing if the sick are not present; then if they are not healed instantly, we will not be embarrassed."

We have limited God! We've made Him small and powerless in our eyes. We have watered down His Word in our lives; we have diluted His healing mes-sage and forgotten that "Jesus Christ is the same yesterday, today, and forever" (Heb. 13:8), and that Exodus 15:26 says, ". . . I am the Lord who heals you."

Our own family has received divine healing many times. There were other times when we felt directed to use doctors. We should allow God to choose the way He wants to heal us.

Ed was healed instantly a few years ago of pneumonia. The doctor had sent him home with in-structions to stay in bed for at least ten days. He would have put him in the hospital, but all the beds were taken. Ed had fainted the night before from the pain of the fluid in his lungs. The Lord impressed him to call a minister to pray with him over the phone, and as the minister prayed, the tightness, pain, congestion, and deep cough were suddenly gone! Ed got up out of bed, came downstairs, ate dinner, and went back to work the next morning completely healed.

OUT OF THE VALLEY OF DISEASE

Several years ago, after having had two major surgeries and one minor surgery in less than two years, I was informed by my doctor that more growths had come back into my body. I was completely devastated by the news and the possibility of having additional surgery or radium treatments.

As soon as I arrived home from the doctor's office, I called my husband at work and explained what I had just been told. "Oh, Ed, please pray," I said. Right then over the phone we both agreed, for God's Word says in Matthew 18:19: ". . . if two of you shall agree on earth as touching any thing that they shall ask, it shall be done for them of my Father which is in heaven" (KJV). Ed said simply, "God, heal Betty."

He heard! God heard! Praise the Lord! The very next day additional tests were made by another specialist, who said, "I really don't understand this, but I find no growths whatsoever. They just aren't there."

Excitedly, I said, "Doctor, do you believe in prayer?"

"Yes, I do," he answered.

"Well, this is answered prayer!" I exclaimed.

I might add that this occurred nine years ago, and the growths have never returned.

Yes, God does heal today. Throughout the last few years, we have witnessed countless people who were touched by Jesus and healed of arthritis, heart problems, sinus problems, bursitis, kidney problems, deformed limbs, misaligned backs, gall bladder problems—even cancer.

We have received letters after our meetings that told of people being healed of serious gum disease (and having it confirmed by the dentist), of being healed of hernias (and having it confirmed by their surgeons), of a lady being healed of an ulcer and her internist having the X-rays to prove it.

One woman called to say her son's lungs were completely free of all fungus and disease. The parents had brought him to an inner healing meeting for prayer. He had suffered numerous bouts of pneumonia and severe allergies. The doctors had told the parents, "We have used all available antibiotics on your son, and they are not effective. There is nothing else to use." The Lord healed him that night. When the next X-rays showed absolutely no problem in the lungs, the doctors were as elated as the parents.

In another meeting, while praying for a woman's deep depression, the Lord healed a broken vertebrae in her back. Instantly all pain and discomfort was gone. More important than her physical healing, however, was her spiritual and emotional healing. The pastor's wife observed that she was a totally different woman. Thank You, Jesus, for her miracle.

Whatever the problem, when God heals you, it is a miracle. It is God doing something for us that we cannot do for ourselves.

There was such joy in praying over the phone with a friend who was facing back surgery and listening as she excitedly said, "The Lord has taken away the pain!" She did not have the surgery. Or to pray with a friend's mother-in-law and watch the power of the Lord go through her, almost like electricity, and heal her of an excruciating backache. She is a very reserved lady, but her hands shot up in the air and she exclaimed, "Praise the Lord!"

At a luncheon with two hundred ladies in Canada, the first lady who wanted prayer had an elbow that had been broken and had mended crooked. We all watched in amazement as God straightened her elbow right before our very eyes. The two friends who brought her hugged each other and literally leaped for joy, examining and re-examining the straightened elbow. There was no doubt for all who watched. God does heal today!

I still recall with amazement a young teacher whose face was covered with acne. She had spent a tremendous amount of money and time going to dermatologists, but the Lord healed her supernaturally in just a few days.

One of our most precious memories is of a young couple who had a baby with congenital heart problems. When he was born, the parents had been told that they might never be able to take him home from the hospital. They couldn't even get him strong enough for surgery.

We prayed with the mother over the phone and again outside the window of the intensive care unit where the baby lay. Many prayers were lifted up for this baby. Gradually, that little one began to improve. Then came the day he was allowed to go home, and they brought him over for prayer. We placed him on a blanket on the floor and knelt beside him, forming a loving prayer circle, asking the Lord for a miracle.

That's exactly what God performed—a miracle. When I talked to the mother later, the doctor had reported that the baby's heart problem was gone. The child was healthy; and to the delight and amazement of all, the mother was giving him swimming lessons! Praise the Lord!

God is the only one who can heal, and we give all the

praise and glory to Him. How thankful we are to be able to witness some of the beautiful things that He does. There is no way you can humanly explain how He can instantly heal. We just know that He can!

With all our hearts we believe God is pouring out His Spirit today. We believe He does heal today, but not in every instance the way we expect. And, yes, there are those who are not healed here on earth, but whom God takes to be with Him. That is the perfect and final healing.

THERE MUST BE A BALANCE

This chapter may cover some of the questions you've asked about healing. We've tried to answer them as honestly as we know how. Unfortunately, there have been some people who have thrown out the entire idea that God heals today because not all of their questions have been answered concerning divine healing, or because they prayed and were not healed instantly.

We must add that there has been occasional misuse of the teaching, "Just claim your healing and you're healed," or "Confess it and you'll possess it." There must be a balance. I rode in a car on the freeway with a lady one day who shared, "I'm claiming healing for my eyes, and I've taken off my glasses. As of yet I can't see, but I'm still claiming my healing." This was not *faith* but *presumption*. The miracle in this instance was that God got us home safely without an accident! She has since put her glasses on again.

Yes, we're to have faith to move mountains. Yes, we're to have positive confession. Yes, we are to believe, and yes, we are to speak the Word. But until God does heal, He intends for us to use our common sense and wear our glasses, take the heart medicine, or the insulin shots, or whatever is needed. *We always urge people to have their doctors verify their healing before stopping medication.*

I recall sharing on inner healing in one out-of-state meeting, when a lady was pushed up in a wheelchair. She was not asking for physical healing, but emotional healing. She said, "I feel so depressed and defeated. A minister recently told me that I wasn't healed because either I didn't have enough faith or I didn't *want* to be well." She continued her story: "I've had polio since I was a child and have been in a wheelchair since that time. My legs are like match stems."

That night she was not healed physically, but I praise God that through the prayer for inner healing she *was* set free from the added burden of the false guilt that she had been carrying.

Many years ago, shortly before I had surgery to remove a tumor, a well-meaning lady said, "If you just had more faith, that tumor would go away." Her statement did not instill confidence or hope in me; it made me feel guilty. I was walking in the amount of light I had at that time. I had neither been taught the Scriptures on healing, nor read books on miracles, nor listened to testimonies of people who had been healed. I went home that night feeling like a very weak Christian and a second-rate person. I felt it was all my fault because I didn't have enough faith to be healed.

I believe in positive confession with all my heart, but we must never intimidate people so that they are afraid to ask for prayer and feel guilty because they are sick.

If you have doubted that divine healing occurs today, if you have prayed and were not healed, if you are sick even as you read this; I pray that God will illuminate His Word and His truths to you. Remember: God loves you, He knows all about you, and He cares. I fervently pray that you will receive the healing you need — in spirit, soul, or body — even as you read this book.

HOW MUCH FAITH IS NEEDED TO BE HEALED?

"Is it just those with tremendous faith who are healed?" you may ask. No, not always. The Bible tells us, ". . . If you had faith even as small as a tiny mustard seed . . . Nothing would be impossible" (Matt. 17:20). God's Word says that even a small amount of faith can accomplish great things. Kathryn Kuhlman told the story of a reporter who came to her meeting as an agnostic, and the Lord touched and healed him physically and spiritually.

A lady came up for prayer one night for her stomach problems, which included multiple gallstones and a spastic colon. Her attitude was "What have I got to lose?" With that small amount of faith, the Lord healed her. Here is her heart-warming letter:

> Over a period of years, everything was done for me that could be done medically, including surgery and various prescriptions, but I continued to have a great deal of pain. I was afraid to go out in public, because I never knew if I would have an attack of pain. When I learned that you would soon be conducting a meeting at our church, I began to eagerly anticipate this meeting.

After it was over and the altar call was given for those who wanted prayer, I just sat there shaking. I asked myself, "What have I got to lose?" The answer was, "Nothing."

With this thought, I gathered enough courage to step forward and seek prayer.

Soon afterward, I experienced a dramatic improvement emotionally and physically. Three months later, my doctor dismissed me as totally recovered. Only Jesus, the greatest Physician of all, could heal both the emotional cause and the physical effects of my illness. Praise His name!

I've heard Father Robert DeGrandis, a Catholic priest with an anointed healing ministry, say to an audience, "Don't ever, ever, ever, ever, *ever,* say to someone, 'You don't have enough faith or you'd be healed.'" When it is put that strongly, it makes a lasting impression on you.

It is not the amount of faith, but God's love and mercy, that heals.

PRAY FOR ANOTHER
THAT YOU MIGHT BE HEALED

James 5:16 says, "Admit your faults to one another and pray for each other so that you may be healed. . . ." There are times when a person stands praying for another, and he himself is healed. After an inner healing meeting, a woman came up and asked for prayer for her daughter, who at that time was going through a traumatic divorce. The mother wrote later:

As I stood there, I felt my eye being healed. I had suffered a hemorrhage in my left eye and was told that I had herpes in the eye. We spent a small fortune going to three ophthalmologists and a neurosurgeon, but the pain was still there. I even spent ten days in the hospital taking Demerol. When I came to the meeting, I was still taking codeine every day for the pain.

As I stood asking prayers for my daughter, my eye began to burn as if it would go out of my head. Well, my eye was wonderfully healed, and I even have better vision than I had at the time the ailment began. My husband and I give God praise.

We have witnessed this all across the country. Many, many times when people ask for prayer for another, forgetting about their own pain and suffering, they themselves are healed.

GOD IS NOT A BELLHOP

There are many different beliefs when it comes to divine healing. Personally, I believe that all physical and emotional healing is divine. I praise the Lord for Christian doctors, nurses, psychologists, and psychiatrists, but they will be the first to tell you that they cannot heal; they only treat. *God* heals. And He can heal naturally through doctors and medicine or supernaturally through prayer.

But there are other times when a Christian is struck with an illness and all the praying, anointing with oil, and praise does not bring healing. The pain does not leave; the cancer returns. But God is sovereign. We cannot put strings on Him and demand that He heal us right when we want it.

OUT OF THE VALLEY OF DISEASE

In *Adventures in Prayer* Catherine Marshall quoted a friend as saying that she "had a special horror of prayers which treated the Lord of the Universe as a bellhop or celestial Santa Claus."* He cannot be treated as such.

Once we were asked by a minister who was skeptical of miracles happening today, "But what about all the people who are not healed at those giant healing services?" My husband answered, "How many must be healed to make it worthwhile to pray?" Of course the answer is *just one*! We keep sharing the Good News that Jesus lives and that He promises us life eternal if we accept Him as Lord and Savior. If just *one* precious soul finds the Lord when we share, it's worth it all! Likewise, if just *one* person is healed when we pray, it is worth all the prayers that have been lifted up.

There are many avenues to healing, but they should all lead to God; for all healing ultimately comes from God. People are healed through medical skill, surgery, and medicines. They may also be healed by getting rid of negative emotions: guilt, unforgiveness, bitterness, hate. Healing may come through a change of climate, diet, or job. God usually will not do for us what we can do for ourselves. But we should go to Him first of all when we are sick and ask, "God, how do you want to heal me?" God does not heal every time the way we expect, and there are certain conditions to be met (these will be mentioned later). We cannot manipulate Him, but I do believe He would like for us to walk in divine health.

*From *Adventures in Prayer*. Copyright © 1975 by Catherine Marshall. Published by Chosen Books, Inc., Lincoln, Virginia. Used by permission.

YOU'VE GOT TO BE KIDDING

The lengthening of arms and legs causes more questioning, more raised eyebrows, and more skepticism than most other healings. Can a leg actually grow out? "No!" says the non-Christian. "No," says the doubting Thomas. "Well, *maybe* it is possible with God, but not probable in this day and time," he concludes. Even from your Christian friends you may get the response, "You've got to be kidding!"

Frankly, I don't know how God lengthens a leg or arm, or as some say, adjusts the spine; I only know I have seen Him do so. I don't know if He relaxes the muscles which allows the leg to stretch; I don't know if He realigns the spine; I don't know if He actually "grows" the bone. All I know is that we have seen people limp up for prayer and walk away normally after the Lord touched and healed them.

One young minister cannot explain how legs grow out, either. But he *can* tell you that since he was run over by a car when he was five, he had walked with a limp and had suffered from pain. He *can* tell you how it felt to be teased and laughed at while he was growing up because of his severe limp. He *can* tell you of the agony and embarrassment he felt as he limped across a stage to receive his diploma. His leg had been broken in several places in the accident; his back had been affected also. There were pinched nerves which caused severe pain and affected his entire nervous system. He can also tell you that God touched him, made his legs the same length, and took away all his back pain. He was able to discard his built-up shoe, and he dismissed plans for pending surgery. How did God do it? I don't know! The young man doesn't know, either. He just knows that *God did it,* and he praises Him for it.

One day in our office a skeptical newspaper reporter who was reviewing this part of the book said, "You know, I've never seen the Lord lengthen a leg." Immediately the Holy Spirit impressed me that she, too, had a short leg. We had her sit in a straight chair, with her back firmly against the back of the chair. To her amazement, one leg was an inch shorter than the other. To her added amazement, she watched the Lord lengthen the leg until they were both the same length. She stood up and said, "You know, my back feels funny." We said one more prayer: "God, please take away that 'funny' feeling." She walked back to the typewriter a firm believer that God does perform miracles, and that ". . . signs shall follow them that believe . . ." (see Mark 16:17–20 KJV).

A Women's Aglow president called the day after one of our meetings with joyful news. A Baptist Sunday school teacher who had been at the meeting was calling all over town sharing her miracle, the very first miracle she had ever seen.

At the close of the meeting the Lord had impressed me that someone was being healed of a hip problem, but no one acknowledged the healing. However, when the meeting was over, a delightful little lady came up to Ed and with some embarrassment said, "I think I was the one the Lord touched."

"Is all the pain gone?" he asked.

"Yes," she said, "it is."

"You have a short leg also, don't you?" he asked. She looked down at her feet, as if to say, "No, both feet are touching the floor."

Ed had her sit in a chair. A group from her Sunday school class watched while he prayed. As her leg "grew out" her arms shot up and she said for the first time, "Praise the Lord."

The ladies standing by their teacher praised God with her. They had just witnessed that God still performs miracles—and believe it or not, He actually can lengthen a leg.

DOES SIN ALONE CAUSE DISEASE?

If a person has consumed enormous amounts of liquor all his life, he is likely to develop cirrhosis of the liver. If a person continues to smoke several packages of cigarettes daily and refuses to listen to medical warnings that they do cause cancer, he may indeed develop cancer of the lungs, throat, or mouth. Venereal disease is spread primarily by illicit sex.

The individual who allows the sins of hatred, an unforgiving attitude, and bitterness to permeate his system will find that those negative emotions are similar to poison and acid: They eat away at the lining of the stomach and colon.

Someone has said, "Sin always causes disease, either spiritual, emotional, or physical, but all disease does not necessarily come from sin."

In some Christian groups, people are taught that sickness is the result of sin that has not been dealt with. If a member is sick, the question is insinuated, "What have you done to cause this illness?" The person is then burdened not only with the sickness, but also with guilt and condemnation.

In John 9:2,3 Jesus was asked, ". . . 'Why was this man born blind? Was it a result of his own sins or those of his parents?' 'Neither,' Jesus answered. 'But to demonstrate the power of God. . . .' " We must never pull self-righteous cloaks around ourselves and point fingers, or probe to see what sin our sick friend has committed.

If you are sick and there is sin in your life that you know brought on your illness, confess it, repent, ask forgiveness, and ask God to heal you. If there is no *known* sin, don't let Satan put guilt or condemnation on you by insinuating that you're being punished by God for some hidden, evil deed.

Silas could have asked Paul as they both were in chains in prison, bleeding, bruised, aching and in pain, "What sin did you commit, Paul, to cause this to happen to us? Surely there must be some deep, unconfessed sin in your life."

However, this was not the case. God had something glorious in store; and as they loudly praised and worshipped the Lord, the miracles began to take place.

So, we as Christians must never condemn the sick and suffering. Perhaps they are reaping the consequences of sin, but that may not be the case. God may be allowing their strong faith to be tested, as an example to others that we can be victorious and overcomers *even in sickness and suffering*—even when we are in the valley.

WHAT BLOCKS HEALING?

At the close of a meeting, a lady asked me to pray for her back and sciatic nerve. Even as she talked, she kept rubbing her back gingerly. I could tell she was in pain. "It just bothers me so much," she said. She paused and added as an afterthought, "I also want you to pray for my husband; he's not a Christian."

Then she went into detail explaining all the things he did wrong. Her face was filled with resentment, and I sensed she needed to do some forgiving. She ended her treatise with, "He is the thorn in my flesh."

I must admit the thought flashed through my mind, "I wonder how much the pain in her back is caused by the resentment over her husband being the 'thorn' in her flesh?" I remember with heaviness that she would not forgive her husband, and she walked away with the pain still in her back.

In Psalm 37:7,8, God's Word tells us, "Rest in the Lord; wait patiently for him to act. . . . Stop your anger! Turn off your wrath. Don't fret and worry—it only leads to harm. . . ." Surely some of the harm God is talking about is the physical harm that anger and resentment causes in our own bodies.

In an out-of-state meeting, another lady was healed of a long-standing back problem because she *did* forgive. She shared that she had been in a car accident nineteen years earlier and had never completely forgiven the person responsible for the wreck. Her total healing had been blocked. She received much healing at the meeting when God touched her back.

But it was when she was home alone and she finally said, "God I forgive the person who caused the accident," that her healing was completed. She said that her back "cracked" and "popped" all the way up and down her spine. She was completely healed after she forgave. She shared a year later in another meeting that she was still completely free of pain.

The Lord wants us to be whole in spirit, soul, and body. "He was wounded and bruised for our sins. He was chastised that we might have peace; he was lashed—and we were healed!" (Is. 53:5). Surely He knows that every area of our lives has to be in balance and harmony before we can experience wholeness. If one area is out of line, our healing may be blocked or delayed.

Father Robert DeGrandis, a Catholic priest, has written an excellent booklet on forgiveness, *Forgiveness Is Healing*. In his book *Introduction to the Healing Ministry* he lists some blocks to spiritual healing: (1) Unbelief, (2) Demanding our own terms, (3) Pride, (4) Insufficient instruction, and (5) Iniquity.* He believes ninety percent of all sickness may relate to unforgiveness. A healing may be blocked by not forgiving either ourselves, others, or God.

Unbelievable as it seems, there are some people who do not want to be healed, because subconsciously they feel that their illness is the only thing keeping a husband from leaving or a son from leaving home to marry.

Is it any surprise that a child may not be able to overcome asthma when we learn of his horrible home life with an alcoholic father who continually beats him?

Introduction to the Healing Ministry by Father Robert DeGrandis, S.S.J., © 1974, pp. 21-22. Used by permission.

His unbearable circumstances may be blocking his healing.

We block wholeness and health when we continually abuse our bodies with overwork and neglect, with overeating or undereating, or by not exercising or taking time for relaxation.

SHOULD WE PRAY MORE THAN ONCE?

Some people believe that you should pray once and only once for an ailment and then trust God for your healing, even though you may still have the symptoms. However, I don't believe it is a lack of faith to keep praying. The Bible tells us in Ephesians 6:18 to "Pray all the time. Ask God for anything in line with the Holy Spirit's wishes. Plead with him, reminding him of your needs. . . ." If you recall, in Mark 8:22–25, even Jesus laid his hands on the blind twice.

Jesus told his disciples the story about the widow who kept going before the judge to remind him of her need. Likewise, God will give justice to His people who plead with Him day and night (see Luke 18:1–7). God has an appointed time for us to be healed. Until then, I believe we should keep praying, unless the Lord tells us specifically not to do so and gives the assurance that the person is healed indeed.

We were in Canada staying in the home of a well-known orthopedic surgeon. He and his wife are beautiful Christians. Unfortunately, he had broken his toe and it was very painful. They had prayed; others had prayed. But God's Word says to pray without ceasing. When Ed was asked to anoint him with oil and pray, he did so, and asked again that God heal that broken toe.

OUT OF THE VALLEY OF DISEASE

A letter from the doctor's wife revealed that when new X-rays were taken two days later, the toe was healed perfectly.

My husband had his toe X-rayed before we left on our vacation. In spite of intermittent pain, the X-rays showed a *perfect healing* — as if there had been no fractures at all. Praise the Lord! I believe that the enemy was trying to make him believe that he had not been healed, when in reality, God had healed him when you prayed.

I was visiting a small, newly organized church one Sunday. During the service, one of the men had to get up and walk around, because his back was hurting so severely. While I was chatting with the man's wife after the service, the Lord seemed to impress me that He wanted to heal the man. The friend and her husband came that afternoon for prayer. He walked in very slowly, and stiffly eased himself into a straight chair, obviously very much in pain.

The man shared that when he was three years old, a big console radio had fallen on him, breaking the femur bone. The bone was set, but later X-rays showed the set had slipped. So, they had to do surgery and put a silver plate in his leg.

When he was eleven, he was playing football and suffered another break where the plate was. At this time, they had to put in silver rings to strengthen and reinforce the leg. After the bone was healed, the rings were removed. Later he suffered from overgrowth, and one leg grew longer than the other. Because of this problem, when he was about twenty-two he had to have surgery again to remove a piece of the bone in an attempt to make the legs even. But even after surgery, there was still a difference in length.

He suffered no more pain until one month earlier, when he was helping to push a compact car. The strain caused a pinched nerve in his back. He said that the pain was so excruciating it almost knocked him to his knees.

That afternoon we anointed him with oil and prayed, asking the Lord to realign his back and lengthen his leg. Praise God! He did just that! Then we prayed that all the pain would leave. When we finished the prayer, we asked, "How is your back?"

He stood up very, very carefully. "Well," he said, "the test is in sitting back down." And very slowly he sat down, stood up, and then said, "You know, I believe it's better." We prayed again, asking the Lord to touch the muscles and nerves and to align the back.

"Now, test it again." He stood up and twisted his back all around. "It's better. It really is." His wife had tears in her eyes as we watched God perform His divine healing.

We prayed one more time. This time when we had finished praying, he left the room for a moment; when he came back he was carrying the back brace he had been wearing.

We all joined in thanking the Lord for what He had done. Then a peculiar thing happened. That night the pain came back worse than ever. But the man stood firm in the knowledge that God had healed him. The next day all pain was completely gone, and it has not returned. That was over four years ago. That afternoon we prayed not just once, but several times before the pain left.

OUT OF THE VALLEY OF DISEASE

In *The Power to Heal,* the author shares his experience with "soaking prayer."

I have been teaching people to pray the soaking prayer; for parents to pray for their children; for husbands and wives to pray for each other for all those longtime, deep-down sicknesses that have not responded to briefer prayers. Ailments, such as mental retardation, that are rarely healed in an instant, now seem to be notably improved and occasionally healed by means of parents soaking the child in prayer over a period of months or years. . . . I find it helps to think of soaking prayer as being like radiation or X-ray therapy.*

DOES GOD EVER DELAY A HEALING?

There are times when we have done everything we know; yet we are not healed at that particular time. I recall the time several years ago when we were to help minister at a service. The morning of the meeting I woke up with a migraine headache. Before Ed left for work, he prayed for me and anointed me with oil. The headache did not go away but continued to get worse. I did everything I knew to do. I bound Satan in the name of Jesus. I forgave everyone I could think of. I asked forgiveness of anything and everything I could think of that might be blocking my healing. I tried praying, singing, and praising. I stood on God's promises and quoted Scriptures, but the headache did not go away.

My husband called midday to say, "Don't take

The Power To Heal by Francis MacNutt, O.P. (Notre Dame, Indiana: Ave Maria, 1977), pp. 42–43. Used by permission.

anything for the pain. Let's trust the Lord to heal you."
By afternoon, I was in sheer agony. Other friends had
prayed with me during the day. When Ed got home
from work, he prayed again. Later, at the beginning of
the meeting, the evangelist prayed for me. Still, the
headache persisted. By this time, I was deathly sick.
But I had gone to the meeting determined that Satan
was not going to have the victory. I knew the price had
been paid on the cross by Jesus, and by His stripes I was
healed (see 1 Peter 2:24 KJV).

At the close of the meeting, the first person who
came to the altar for prayer was a person with a
headache. I thought, "Well, praise the Lord. I will pray
for her, and in the process, my own headache will go
away." ("Pray for each other so that you may be
healed . . ." is what God's Word says in James 5:16.)
The Lord took away her headache instantly, but mine
was twice as bad.

The next person was a lady with severe allergy
problems. I thought, "Oh, thank you, Lord. This time,
surely when I pray for her, You will honor the prayer
and also heal me at the same time." After prayer, the
lady said, "I haven't felt this good in twenty years."
And what about my headache? By this time, I was so
sick at my stomach and in such pain, I thought, "I can't
stand this much longer."

The third person at the altar was a young woman
who said, "I have an excruciating headache; I've been
told by the doctor that I have a brain tumor." I
thought, "Lord, *surely* this is why I have had such a
headache. Satan did not want this woman to be
healed." So we prayed asking the Lord Jesus to take
away her headache, and He did immediately. (Later

we learned that new X-rays showed there was no tumor.) Praise the Lord!

And how was my head? It was throbbing as it had never throbbed before, and my stomach was in such a state, I thought I would "up-chuck" at any moment. When the meeting was over, we went home with me holding my poor, pounding head.

Perhaps you have never been in this state of affairs, but I want to be completely honest with you. I was angry at God. I felt sorry for myself. I had done everything I knew to do in order to "claim" my healing. I had tried to meet all the conditions, and I had only continued to grow worse. Even after taking the strongest medication available that night after we got home, the headache still did not go away.

I began to murmur to the Lord and ask, *"Why?"* I slept very little that night. I woke the next morning, and as you might suspect, my head was still throbbing, and I was still murmuring. I had stopped praising the Lord hours earlier.

Then something very unusual happened. That morning at 10:00, I felt as if someone tapped me on the shoulder, and I heard that inner voice of the Lord say, *Betty.*

"Yes, Lord."

If I never took away your headache, would you still pray for the sick?

I was shattered as I stood before the Lord. I knew my answer immediately, and with a contrite and humbled heart, I said, "Oh, Lord, You know I would." Immediately my headache vanished.

I would love to tell you I have never had another headache, but I have. On occasions when we aren't healed immediately, those are the times to "Trust in the Lord with all thine heart; and lean not unto thine own understanding" (Prov. 3:5 KJV). I think the Lord was teaching me that we should pray for the sick whether we feel like it or not. We should continue to praise God, even if He doesn't heal us instantly.

I am aware that the experience I have described was only a one-night episode of endurance. I know that this is minor compared to what some people go through. There are people who suffer pain day-in, day-out — night after night of unrelenting, agonizing pain. They too have stood on God's promises, praised God, quoted Scripture, prayed and prayed and prayed. But the medication does not annihilate the giant of pain, the surgery does not kill the foraging monster of cancer.

> We ask, "Why, Lord?"
> There are no pat answers.
> Our only recourse is still,
> "God, I trust You and I praise You."

THE THREE TYPES OF HEALING:
SPIRIT, SOUL, BODY

The most important healing of all is *spiritual healing*. We have heard our good friend, Captain John LeVrier, say so many times that if he had to choose between his physical healing of terminal cancer at a Kathryn Kuhlman meeting and the spiritual healing that came with the baptism in the Holy Spirit, he would choose the latter, because at least he would die happy.

44

There is not one thing we can do to change the color of our eyes or to add one inch to our height. God wants us to be happy just the way He made us. He desires that we respect His handiwork, take care of it, and praise Him for it.

"Haven't you yet learned that your body is the home of the Holy Spirit God gave you, and that He lives within you? Your own body does not belong to you. For God has bought you with a great price. So use every part of your body to give glory back to God, because He owns it" (1 Cor. 6:19,20).

Although we cannot change our bodies, we can change our attitudes. Many times when we get our attitudes right, we will be healed physically. We have seen the Lord perform inner healing, and yet not complete physical healing at that time.

While speaking to one group of ladies, I encouraged them to go home, look in the mirror, and say, "Thank you, Lord, for making me just the way You did. I love You, and I love myself." At the close of the meeting, a lady came up for prayer. She was partially paralyzed on one side from a stroke. Her arm dangled at her side, and she walked with a slight limp. While she was telling me, "So many people have prayed for my physical healing, and I have not been healed," the Lord was telling me that He wanted to heal her on the *inside* first. We prayed for inner healing for her, and as the power of the Lord came upon her, it brought a radiant glow to her face.

Some time later, I received a long letter from her. It must have been hard for her to write because her hand was still semi-paralyzed, but oh, the joy of that letter.

Betty, I did what you told me to do. I went home, determined to praise God for my condition. I went into the bathroom where there is a full-length mirror. Always before, I hated to look into that mirror and see my face. I felt so ugly. But that day, as I started to look into the mirror, I heard the Lord say, "When you look into your eyes, you will see Me." Oh, glory! That is exactly what happened!

She did not see her body in its paralysis. She saw Jesus. She continued in her letter, "Now people come up to me and say, 'Oh, you're so beautiful!'" And she truly is. She has the love of Jesus all over her face, especially in her eyes. She wrote in one of her letters, "I'm healed on the inside, and that's what is important. I feel like I'm standing up on the inside." What a blessing she is to others.

One night we were praying with a teacher and his family. The wife shared that she had a fear of not being able to breathe. While we were praying for her, the Holy Spirit revealed to me that at birth the umbilical cord had been wrapped around her neck. (Of course the lady did not remember this experience and had never been told anything about it by her mother.) We prayed that the Lord would heal that buried memory of not being able to breathe at birth.

When she asked her mother later on, the mother said, "Yes, the umbilical cord was around your neck; in fact you almost died at birth." This lady had suffered seizures all her life at the rate of two or three a week. Perhaps they came from this birth injury; but praise the Lord, He healed her of the weekly seizures. Since our prayers she has suffered only two in over a year. God healed her physically and emotionally.

OUT OF THE VALLEY OF DISEASE

In *Set Free,** I shared the story of a boy who was healed of a number of problems, including nightmares and fear of the dark. His broken ankle had been healed also. A tremendous part of his experience was the healing of hypoglycemia (low blood sugar). When we were praying for him, the Lord led me to pray for a proper chemical balance in his system. His parents shared later that he had been healed completely of this disease. We received this testimony from his mother:

At the advice of a fine Christian doctor, we took our two-and-a-half-year-old son to a psychiatrist. He was diagnosed as a hyperkinetic child. From age two to seven, our family went through trying times as his body began to level off in the treatment. Those who have a hyperactive child know the stress and anxiety this causes.

After five years of treatment and regular visits to the psychiatrist, our son was reported to be a well boy. But he was to remain on the treatment for life. He still suffered from fears and feelings of inadequacy. From the time he was two years old he suffered from the fear of sleeping alone and the fear of the dark.

The day we prayed with you, the Lord healed our son's fears, corrected his chemical imbalance and He also filled him with His Holy Spirit. He was healed spiritually, emotionally, and physically by God.

DO I HAVE TO HAVE SOMEONE PRAY WITH ME?

Absolutely not! It is God who heals. Of course, I

Set Free by Betty Tapscott (Houston: Hunter Publishing Co., 1978), p. 96.

encourage you to have someone agree with you because God's Word says, ". . . if two of you agree down here on earth concerning anything you ask for, my Father in heaven will do it for you" (Matt. 18:19). But remember, God is your source, and all eyes should be on Him.

Even though it is God who heals, He *does* allow people to be His channels of healing. He does not need our help, but out of His goodness and grace, He lets each of us be a part of His healing power at different times. He will not, however, share His glory!

At the end of an inner healing seminar, Ed voiced what the Lord was saying to him: Someone was being healed of a heart problem. A lady came forward saying all of her pain and discomfort were gone. She was a heart patient at a hospital and had asked to be released to come to the meeting. *No one prayed with her.* God alone touched and healed her. The next night, the Lord impressed Ed that He was healing someone of cancer in the esophagus area—and to the amazement of us all, the same lady came forward. She had tumors in this area. The doctor had said that he would have to use radium to dissolve them, but God did it supernaturally.

The third night of the meetings, the Lord impressed us that someone's elbow was being healed. After the meeting was over, this same precious lady came up saying all the pain was gone in her elbow. She said, "I didn't come up during the meeting because I was afraid everyone would think I was a hypochondriac." God healed her of three different ailments, and no one laid hands on her or prayed for her.

OUT OF THE VALLEY OF DISEASE

In another inner healing meeting, a lady was healed while she sat in the audience. She was a Disciples of Christ pastor's wife and had suffered pain in her right side for years. When the Lord revealed to Ed that He was healing someone with a knot on the right side, she came forward. The pain had been so severe that she wondered if it were cancer. God touched and healed her without anyone praying with her.

One of the most tremendous testimonies I have ever heard told how God reached down to touch a young man lying in a hospital room all alone.

While he was in college studying voice, the man was involved in a horrible car accident. His entire face from the nose down was crushed, and his vocal cords were severed. He could not speak, much less sing. For nine months he was in the hospital, undergoing plastic surgery.

One day the young man heard the song, "He Touched Me", on the radio. Silently he cried out to the Lord, asking Him to heal him, and God did *instantly*! As he felt the power of the Lord flow through him, he exclaimed, "Well, praise the Lord!" A nurse coming through the door was so astonished she dropped her tray. This young man surrendered his life to the Lord to preach and sing for Him. When we met him years later, he said, "I'm a firm believer in inner healing because God healed all my painful memories of this accident. He set me free from the agonizing nightmares of the wreck that had plagued me, and healed every painful memory." God healed him when he was all alone. It is God who heals. *He* is our source!

DOES GOD WANT *ME* TO PRAY
FOR THE SICK?

After we have come out of a valley experience—or even while we are there—God wants to use us as a guide to lead others. Sometimes when people can't trust, praise, or pray, God wants us to do it for them.

God uses people on this earth to do His work. Yes, He wants to use each of us. I'm not saying we are to go up to a sick person, corner her and pray for her whether she wants it or not. But when He sends someone to us and she asks for prayer or mentions a need, by all means offer to pray. "But what if she isn't healed?" you ask. Not everyone accepts Jesus as Savior, but we keep on sharing the Good News. Likewise not everyone is healed when we pray, but we are to keep on praying. If they are healed, praise the Lord! If they are not healed, it still is in God's hands. Our job is to share the Good News that Jesus heals. It's His business to heal in the manner He chooses.

What Christian mother has not voiced a prayer for a critically ill baby: "Oh God, please heal, please take away my baby's pain and fever." We don't have to *understand* the theology of healing. We just need to remember that our heavenly Father is a loving Father. You can come before Him not only with your pain, but also with your questions.

You may say: "But my church doesn't believe that God heals today," or "My denomination doesn't practice the laying on of hands," or "My family would think I had flipped if I asked someone to anoint me with oil," or "I'm not sure that I even believe that God heals."

50

OUT OF THE VALLEY OF DISEASE

Several years ago, I did not know about miracles or the Scriptures on healing. I had been baptized in the Holy Spirit for only two days when I was asked to substitute for a teacher whose son was terminally ill with leukemia. When the principal of the elementary school called, she said, "I want you to be ready to take over her class." So, I went to the school to train as her replacement.

It was during the physical education class for the second-graders that I heard myself saying to the teacher whose son had leukemia, "I believe in miracles."

In surprise, she answered, "You do?" In astonishment I thought, *I do?* Then I came forth with another statement which surprised me: "I believe in anointing with oil." (I had never said that before!)

"You do?" she responded in amazement.

And silently I asked God, *I do?* Then I added, "I believe God wants to heal your little boy."

"Oh! Where can we take him for prayer and anointing with oil?" she asked with excitement.

I did not know of a church at that time that anointed with oil. But she had a friend who did, and they took the little boy to that church a few days later. The elders prayed according to James 5:14,15, "Is anyone sick? He should call for the elders of the church and they should pray over him and pour a little oil upon him, calling on the Lord to heal him. And their prayer, if offered in faith, will heal him, for the Lord will make him well. . . ."

He was healed. Nine years later he is still in perfect health.

BUT WHAT ABOUT ME?

You may be in a valley of illness at this time. You may be suffering from pain right now. Your mind may be filled with doubts and questions about healing. You may not know what the Scriptures say. Your body may be crippled with arthritis. You may be lying in a hospital bed feeling lonely, hopeless, and depressed. God loves you. He does care! You may be suffering from what the doctors call a terminal illness. God is the God of miracles. Don't give up!

You say, "I'm sick. I've prayed, and I've been prayed for. Why hasn't God healed me? Why does He even allow sickness anyway? Why?" It's the age-old question of suffering. As I've said before, I don't even pretend to have the answer. But this I believe with all my heart: God wants us to keep on praying, praising, and trusting.

Please know you are not alone. I don't understand why some things happen, but I do know that *God loves you.* He wants you to reach out and touch Him. His healing power can go through you even as you are reading this page. Don't lose hope. Keep your eyes on the Lord Jesus. Trust Him, love Him, and praise Him as you walk through the valley of disease.

A PRAYER FOR THE SICK
(Make this your own personal prayer.)

"God, I thank You for knowing me as a special person. You know when I'm sick and in pain. You know when I'm standing by watching members of my family suffer. I don't understand Your ways, but I know You are a just and loving God, and I love and praise You.

"I thank You that you have forgiven all my sins. And I forgive each person who has hurt me in any way. If negative emotions have caused this sickness, please set me free from them: from fear, hatred, resentment, or unforgiveness. I bind Satan from me in the name of Jesus. I bind the spirits of pain and infirmity in the name of Jesus.

"God, please go to the root cause of this sickness and set me free from that problem; heal every painful memory. Touch every nerve and fiber of my body. Renew every damaged cell. Fill me with new strength and health.

"Thank You for Your ministering angels, for the presence of the Holy Spirit. Lord, I know You are with me when I'm sick and discouraged. You are with me in the hospital room, in the mental ward, or at home. Let me feel Your presence, Your love, Your gentle touch. Let me hear Your loving voice. I pray for a miracle, Lord. Let Your healing power flow through me right now in my spirit, soul, and body. Fill me with Your peace. It is in the precious name of Jesus I pray. Amen."

SCRIPTURES ON HEALING

Jeremiah 30:17: "I will give you back your health again and heal your wounds. . . ."

1 Peter 2:24: ". . . for his wounds have healed ours!"

James 5:14,15: "Is anyone sick? He should call for the

elders of the church and they should pray over him and pour a little oil upon him, calling on the Lord to heal him. And their prayer, if offered in faith, will heal him, for the Lord will make him well; and if his sickness was caused by some sin, the Lord will forgive him."

Psalm 103:3: "He forgives all my sins. He heals me."

Isaiah 35:5,6: "And when he comes, he will open the eyes of the blind, and unstop the ears of the deaf. The lame man will leap up like a deer, and those who could not speak will shout and sing! . . ."

Mark 16:18: ". . . and they will be able to place their hands on the sick and heal them."

Acts 5:16: "And crowds came . . . bringing their sick folk and those possessed by demons; and every one of them was healed."

Luke 7:20: "The two disciples found Jesus while he was curing many sick people of their various diseases—healing the lame and the blind and casting out evil spirits. . . ."

Psalms 113:9: "He gives children to the childless wife, so that she becomes a happy mother. . . ."

Deuteronomy 7:15: "And the Lord will take away all your sickness. . . ."

Isaiah 53:5: "But he was wounded and bruised for *our* sins. He was chastised that we might have peace; he was lashed—and we were healed!"

3 John 2 (KJV): "Beloved, I wish above all things that thou mayest prosper and be in health, even as thy soul prospereth."

III

OUT OF THE VALLEY
OF GRIEF

Blessed are they that mourn:
for they shall be comforted.

—Matt. 5:4 KJV

My suitcases were packed. I was ready to walk out
the door to catch a plane for a speaking engagement.
The phone rang; it was my parents calling to say that
my grandmother whom I dearly loved, Bittie Mom,
had been taken to the hospital critically ill.

My mind started racing. "Lord, should I cancel the
meeting? Can I rent a private plane and fly home?
What should I do?" Quickly I lifted the situation to the
Lord and asked Him to work out the details. I knew I
couldn't go and minister to others without first going
to be with my family. The first decision was made. We
drove six hours to reach the hospital where my
grandmother lay so terribly ill.

I was at the hospital most of the night. The next day,
with only two hours of sleep, I boarded the plane to my
speaking engagement. I kept praying and singing,
"The Joy of the Lord Is My Strength," and by the time
I arrived at my destination, I felt ten feet tall. For a
five-foot woman, that's something else! The Lord
lifted my burden and my fatigue, and He filled me

with His strength. It was a glorious meeting with many healings, both physical and emotional.

I flew back to the city where my grandmother lay ill and stayed a week with my parents. The doctor said, "I believe your grandmother is stabilizing. She just might get to go home." So, after much prayer asking the Lord to stay His hand, I planned to leave for my next meeting.

Shortly before I left the hospital, Bittie Mom went into terrible pain—bitter agony. We prayed every way we knew. We bound the spirit of pain in the name of Jesus. We prayed for her to be set free from pain. We prayed that the medicine would work. We praised. We did everything we knew to do, but the pain did not subside.

In the midst of this anguish, as my mother and I stood by watching, Bittie Mom raised herself up from the bed. She looked upward, and a glow came over her face. She leaned on one elbow, lifted her other hand, and with awe and excitement, she said, "Oh, look at all the brass beds; I've never seen so many brass beds." The moment was electrifying. There was no doubt in our minds. My mom and I both knew we had been witnesses as one of God's saints caught a glimpse of something to come, something beautiful and glorious.

The Lord had given me peace about leaving again, and my parents and husband encouraged me to keep my speaking engagement. We all felt that it was God's will for me to go.

So again I boarded a plane and soon arrived in the city where I was to speak. Upon reaching my hostess's home, I learned that she had just taken her daughter to the hospital. I had been in the house alone a short time when the phone rang. It was Ed.

"Betty—" By the way he said "Betty" and paused, I knew what he was going to say. "Bittie Mom just died." For a moment, I thought my heart would break. I was overwhelmed with anguish, grief, and anger. I was devastated.

We discussed what I should do. There were no other flights that night. After praying, we both felt the Lord was saying, *I want you to stay and speak in the morning, to glorify Me.*

After we hung up, I felt utterly desolate. Here I was in a strange city and a strange house. Then the devil tried to put guilt on me. *If you were a truly loving granddaughter, you would have stayed at her bedside. Did you really hear the Lord's voice? I thought He said He would stay His hand until you got back. Your poor mother—where were you when she needed you?*

I bound this deceiving spirit in the name of Jesus. I walked around the room with my hands up in the air, saying, "God, I praise You. God, I praise You. I thank You, Lord Jesus. I praise You."

Let me tell you what happened. Within thirty minutes, one of my dearest friends from Houston called to say, "Betty, I'm here in the same city with my husband on vacation. I've felt such a burden for you. I've called back to Houston three times today to find out where you were. I was just told about your grandmother's death."

Look what the Lord did. There I was with my heart aching, full of grief, guilt, and loneliness; and my precious Lord allowed my dearest friend to meet me at the point of my deep need.

Within fifteen minutes, she was at my side. We had ten or fifteen minutes of prayer, and then she left. I was able to go to bed and sleep soundly all night long, really sheltered by His love.

The next morning, as I stood before those ladies to speak, I could praise the Lord and say with assurance, "He *will* heal your broken heart. He *will* bind up your wounds." (See Ps. 147:3.) When you go through sorrow, He will walk through the valley of the shadow of death with you (Ps. 23:4 KJV). You will not have to walk through the valley alone. I have never felt His presence in a more real way. Surely He does send the Comforter to sustain us in our hour of grief.

Bittie Mom's funeral two days later was a glorious praise service. God was lifted up as we celebrated her "graduation."

I wonder how people can go through the loss of a loved one without Jesus, without the promise of life eternal. Because of Jesus and His death on the cross, Christians have the assurance that when death comes they will go to be with Jesus. We know for certain that if our loved ones were Christians, they are with Jesus. They have gone on to something better. They are free from pain. They are completely whole.

But even with the knowledge of heaven, it still is excruciatingly painful to lose a loved one. Only Jesus can heal that hurt. He knows and He cares. He wept when He learned that Lazarus had died, even though He knew Lazarus would be brought back to life. God knew there would be heartache and sorrow. The Bible says that "The Lord lifts the fallen and those bent beneath their loads" (Ps. 145:14).

When there is a deep, deep puncture to our physical

body, the wound is difficult to heal. Grief is like a deep puncture. If the physical wound is free from any foreign matter, it will heal properly without infection. Likewise, if our emotional wound (our grief) is free from the foreign matter of guilt, bitterness, unforgiveness, and anger, and if we allow the oil of the Holy Spirit to flow into the wound, it will heal properly.

However, if a sliver of some foreign matter remains, or the wound isn't cleansed properly, the wound will become infected. There may be an abscess; the wound will become even more painful, sore, and tender.

It's the same with the grief process. If Satan sends guilt, bitterness, anger, revenge, hatred, self-pity, or unforgiveness into the emotional wound and we allow it to remain, the wound becomes infected and will not heal properly. Our grief then becomes abnormal.

A story was related to us of a grandmother, daughter, and grandchild who were still going frequently to the grandfather's grave and kissing his tombstone a year after he had died. This is one form of abnormal grief. Satan had been allowed to keep this family in bondage through uncontrollable grief. When someone grieves this deeply over a death, it may be that the person idolized the one who died. This is a form of idolatry, and God said we shall have no idols. Perhaps the deceased had a higher place than God in this person's life.

Years ago, we were acquainted with a family who lost a young son. The mother kept his room intact, just as it had been before he died. Nothing was allowed to be moved. It is abnormal when life revolves around the dead and not the living. When a person is still crying copious tears years after a loved one has died, then

Satan has shackled the person with the spirit of grief.

The enemy knows when we are hurting, and he takes advantage of these times of sorrow, weakness, and stress to come against us in every possible way. He will try to infect the wound and keep it from healing, in order to keep our eyes on the wound and not on Jesus.

We each have an appointed time to die. Our loved ones have their appointed time, also. Death will come; and when it does, grief will follow. Tears will flow, but they are God's way of cleansing wounds and hastening the healing process.

God will walk through that valley with us. He will hold us in His victorious right hand. He will shelter us. He loves us, and He will send the Comforter to fill the void.

SUICIDE

Of all deaths, perhaps suicide is the hardest to accept. When a loved one commits suicide, the family is left in the throes of doubt and guilt. Each friend or relative asks himself many questions. Why did the person do this? What did I do to cause this? Could I have done something differently to prevent it? Did she suffer long? Did he really mean to kill himself? Will he go to heaven? Did she accept Jesus before she died?

I heard a pastor once say that God is a God of mercy, and he believed if a person had already accepted Jesus as his personal Savior before the satanic spirit of oppression and suicide engulfed him, that he will in death still have God's promise of life eternal. He explained, "The person didn't lose his salvation; but he may have lost his close fellowship with God."

I am aware of the different doctrines proclaiming that, if a person kills himself, he will go to hell; but we have to realize that when a person is distraught enough to do such a thing, he is obviously not in his right mind. We never know for certain what his last thought was. How do we know that he didn't cry out to Jesus in that last moment, "God, forgive me. Jesus, save me!" In no way am I excusing suicide; nor do I mean to give false hope. However, we must not judge the person who is so sick spiritually, emotionally, or physically that he takes his life in a moment of weakness and despair. God is the judge.

It is vital that each person accept Jesus as his Savior. *There is only one way to our Father in heaven, and that is through Jesus.* It is imperative that we stay in Christian fellowship. Then, when we are under an attack of oppression and thinking about self-destruction, the church body can pray for us, and we can be set free. Suicide is caused by satanic oppression, but we have power over Satan. The Bible says, ". . . greater is he that is in you, than he that is in the world" (1 John 4:4 KJV).

A friend and I stood in the emergency room of a hospital by the side of a woman who had just shot herself in the head. Tubes and machines were connected to her entire body. Perhaps, clinically, she was dead; I don't know. But as my friend prayed, "Oh God, forgive her"; as he called her name and told her Jesus loved her and to accept Him as Savior, there was an overpowering, awesome feeling of God's holy presence.

The lady was pronounced dead a short time later. We do not know if she heard him or if she turned her thoughts to Jesus before she died. I believe that even though a person is unconscious, we should talk to him or her about Jesus. We should tell the person to call out to God and ask Jesus for salvation, because the subconscious mind may still be functioning.

Another tragic consequence of suicide is passing on a spiritual inheritance of death and destruction to the children involved. They may be burdened with thoughts such as, "Well, Dad killed himself, so I probably will, too;" or "If Mother thought the best way to solve all her problems was to kill herself, then I'll do the same."

THE EMOTIONS OF GRIEF

Much has been written recently about death and grief, and it is good to discuss it. For ages, people have been afraid to talk about death: their grief, their fears, the anger and guilt.

Once people realize that others have felt the same way; once they realize it's okay to have doubts and ask, "Why, God?"; once they discover that they don't have to feel guilty because the unanswered questions are there, then the healing process can begin.

All our questions will not be answered in this life — the questions of suffering, pain, and death. But if you are grieving, perhaps it will help to know others have felt the same way you feel. An excellent book, *Good Grief*, by Granger Westberg came to my attention some years ago.* It helped me in my understanding of the grief process.

*Copyright 1962, 1971 by Fortress Press.

God wants to walk through each step of that valley with you, cleansing the wounds, healing the painful memories, and setting you free from all the negative emotions that have entered the wound. Grief, like inner healing, is a process.

I CAN'T BELIEVE IT!

When a loved one dies or there is a terrible loss, such as the death of a marriage relationship through divorce, God anesthetizes the initial wound. If he did not do this, the pain and loss might be unbearable. We've all heard people say after a trauma, "I just don't believe it." "It just doesn't seem real." "It seems like a dream."

It is during those first few hours and days of a loss that God supplies a "spiritual pain pill." He applies the oil of the Holy Spirit, the balm of Gilead to those deep, gaping wounds. He gently takes our hand and begins to walk through the valley with us.

It is important to have Scriptures memorized. Then, when you are hurting so badly that you're unable to read, you can draw from the Word hidden in your heart. How beautiful to be able to pray in the Spirit: ". . . for we don't even know what we should pray for, nor how to pray as we should; but the Holy Spirit prays for us with such feeling that it cannot be expressed in words" (Rom. 8:26). If we have endeavored to practice the presence of Jesus,* then in that moment of initial shock and devastating loss when we're knocked to our

---

*See Brother Lawrence's book, *Practice the Presence of God;* there are numerous translations of this Christian classic.

knees, we can know with assurance that He will lift us up.

WHY, GOD, WHY?

Many times, anger and unforgiveness are a part of grief. Bereaved people may be angry at the hospital, the doctor, nurses, or perhaps at other members of the family. The pastor may take the brunt of their feelings, but ultimately God is the object of the anger. "Why, God, why? Why did You allow this to happen? If You're a loving God, where were You when my baby was killed? If You're a God of compassion and gentleness, why did You allow my husband to die?" They vent their fury until finally the storm inside calms and they can hear the still, small voice of God say, *I was there; I was in the same place when My Son died. I do care, and I love you. Please trust Me; let Me heal your hurt.*

At the close of a Catholic prayer meeting where we shared about healing of memories, a young man was brought to us for prayer. He said that when he was sixteen, he was the one who found his mother after she had committed suicide. Oh, the unforgiveness that was buried deep inside of him. He sobbed as if his heart would break. His head dropped into his hands as he asked, "Why did she do it? Why? I can't forgive her for what she did. I can't."

Gently I said, "Oh, don't you know that Satan came against her in a weak, unguarded moment when she could not cope? She did not want to feel depressed and hopeless, but Satan saw his chance and robbed her of physical life. But your *unforgiving attitude* will rob you of your spiritual life. Would you allow Jesus to forgive through you?"

Slowly he said, "God, I do forgive my mother for killing herself." I had him repeat it again. "God, I do forgive my mother for killing herself." Praise the Lord! Those around him watched as God performed a miracle, and His healing power erased the sting, the horror, and the panic of that moment. As God gently cleansed the wound, you could see new life begin to come forth.

The very next night, after a priest shared at our inner healing service that he had to learn not to blame God for allowing his dad to be burned to death, our young friend shared that he had forgiven his mom for taking her own life. The glow on his face revealed that truly there had been deliverance from the bondage of an unforgiving spirit and grief.

We must not harbor guilt if we have anger toward God. We must confess it and ask forgiveness; but we must never forget that God does forgive even our anger towards Him.

If there has been an accident, the person responsible for the accident may be the object of the bereaved's anger. This anger, too, should be confessed to God, otherwise it will begin to fester deep in the wound. If this is the case, the person will need to pray for inner healing.

I recall a meeting several years ago when I prayed with a young widow whose husband had been killed instantly in a car accident a few months before. Suddenly she had become the sole support of four children, and she was filled with bitterness, loneliness, despair, and anger. Her husband had accepted Jesus a short time before his death, for which she was thankful; but still she was completely overwhelmed with grief. She kept asking the Lord, "Why? Why?"

As we were taking authority over the negative emotions that were binding her, I said, "Spirit of grief, you are bound and cast out in the name of Jesus!" There was such an instant release and lifting of oppression that we looked at each other in amazement. At that moment, the Lord cleansed that deep wound of grief and set her free! We see this precious Christian often. Of course, the wound still hurts at times, but God is healing her. And He has recently given her a new Christian husband.

In my book *Inner Healing,* a mother whose son was burned to death testified how God set her free from grief and anger. She was rebellious towards God for allowing her fourteen-year-old son to die in such a horrible way. She and I began to pray, and when the Holy Spirit revealed to us her anger, she lifted her hands to Him and said, "Oh God, please forgive me for my attitude, and for being angry with You for taking Gary."

After praying for inner healing, the power of the Lord fell upon her, and she had a vision of Gary walking hand in hand with Jesus. As she described the beautiful vision of heaven with its vivid green trees and grass, gorgeous flowers, and crystal-clear, shining-blue river, we could almost see it ourselves. Gary, in her vision, was completely healed.

The mother was given such peace and joy that she said, "Oh! I wouldn't bring Gary back to this earth even if I could." Of course, she still has days that are almost unbearable. Her mother's heart was a void, but she has found that God's grace is sufficient to fill it.

IF ONLY I . . .

In the depths of sorrow, when you're weak emotionally, you are very susceptible to Satan's deception. He will try to deceive you by placing guilt on you. He will whisper in your ear, "If only you'd gotten him to the hospital in time. . . ." "If only you had listened to her yesterday when she said she was hurting. . . ." "If you had not asked him to go by the store, he would not have had the wreck." As one wife said, "If only I'd cooked better meals. . . . If only I'd shown more love. . . . If only we hadn't quarreled." Don't let Satan defeat you in this way!

There are times when the feelings of guilt are valid, when there has been a broken relationship that wasn't mended before death, or when a person caused an accident. A measure of comfort can be found in the Scripture, "There is now no condemnation awaiting those who belong to Christ Jesus . . ." (Rom. 8:1). Pray, asking God to set you free from the chain of guilt. Ask the Lord to heal your painful memories, and pray that you can forgive yourself.

Crib deaths in babies (infant death syndrome) is a ghastly experience for parents. Not only do they suffer from the loss of that precious baby, but they are crippled with the feeling of guilt: "If I'd only gotten up to check on him at 2:00. . . ." "If only I hadn't let her cry before she went to sleep. . . ."

If you have gone through that horrible experience,

please remember God knows you are hurting, and He wants to heal that hurt.

A heartbroken teen-age girl came up for prayer at a Christian school where I had just spoken in chapel. She sobbed that she was supposed to have been watching her little sister when the baby accidentally became entangled in a rope and strangled. Oh, the guilt that this teen-ager was carrying! But God is faithful to do just what He said He would do, and He set her free from that bondage. She testified the very next day in chapel that God had delivered her from that horrible guilt. Thank You, Father!

A woman shared her testimony at a meeting of how God healed her of a horrible memory. She had accidentally run over a drunk man and killed him. The horror of the experience haunted her day and night.

She shared the good news though, that two years earlier when I had prayed for healing of memories for her church group, the Lord had set her free. When the meeting was over that night, she had purchased the book, *Inner Healing*. She stayed up all night reading. As she read the book, the Lord continued to cleanse her wounds. He took away all the depression, bitterness, guilt, revenge, hatred, unforgiveness, and self-pity. God healed all the painful memories. And in the process, He also healed her high blood pressure and heart problem. As she stood before her church two years after this experience, she ended her testimony by saying, "Everyone in my church knows that I'm a walking miracle. Isn't that right, pastor?" The pastor sitting on the front row nodded his head in agreement. Praise You, Lord Jesus, for this transformation.

At the close of a meeting where I had spoken on forgiveness, a young lady came to me for prayer. She was sobbing as she said, "My daddy died before I could tell him I was sorry for something I had done. I can't ask his forgiveness. What can I do?"

She stood there with tears streaming down her face. I felt helpless, not knowing what to say. "What do I tell her, Jesus?" I asked. And immediately it seemed that He said, *I'll tell her daddy she is sorry.* Isn't that just like our Lord? Isn't that precious?

Can this be based on theology? I don't know. The only thing I know is that when we agreed in prayer and asked the Lord to set her free from the guilt, He did just that. And when we thanked the Lord for letting her daddy know she was sorry, there was immediate cleansing. She felt forgiven. She had experienced a miracle. She knew that God had done something for her that she could not do for herself.

BEAUTY FOR ASHES

Several years ago I was one of twelve ladies who flew to Belize* in Central America to start a Women's Aglow chapter. At one of the meetings, the Vicar General of the Catholic Diocese of Belize asked me to pray with a young mother. She was dressed in black. Her face was etched deeply with agonizing grief.

Father Castillo shared that a few weeks before, her healthy, normal, two-year-old son had fallen over dead as she was taking him to the park to play. In such a terrifying experience, Satan saw his chance and

*Formerly British Honduras.

wrapped chains of despair, anger, and depression around her.

As we agreed in prayer for healing of memories, our Lord reached down to heal this mother. A year later Father Castillo told us, "She has been such a beautiful witness. She has not allowed this devastating loss to make her bitter, but she has grown by leaps and bounds." She let the Lord give her:

> ". . . Beauty for ashes;
> Joy instead of mourning;
> Praise instead of heaviness. . . ."
> (Is. 61:3)

TRIALS AND SORROWS

In John 16:33 we read, ". . . Here on earth you will have many trials and sorrows. . . ." After a tragedy, a loss, a deep emotional wound, we often hear, "I'm a good person. I'm at church every time the door is open. Is God punishing me? Has he forgotten about me? Why? Why? Why?" No one knows why. No one escapes grief in life. We all have experienced some form of loss, perhaps many different kinds. Death is not the only form of grief and loss.

There are losses and grief in lesser degrees. For example, there is the grief of discovering that a friend has betrayed you or a child has drifted into deep sin; there is the grief that comes from the loss of an eye or an arm or a leg. If we are unable to praise God in all circumstances, we may encounter overwhelming grief with the loss of a job or promotion, the destruction of a life-long dream, loss of a business or life savings, or the loss of a home. A form of grief occasionally comes at retirement time. A severely damaged reputation or being a victim of some hideous crime will cause much grief unless we let Jesus heal the wound. Some suffer a form of grief in life from wanting marriage and children, and remaining single or being childless.

The wounds of divorce may be more difficult to heal than the grief surrounding physical death. If there is a third party who broke up the marriage or if there are children involved, the wound is even deeper and is constantly being reopened.

The loss of a pet may be a child's first encounter with death and may well be a very traumatic experience. At such a time, the child needs more love, compassion, and understanding than ever. Never allow such grief to be minimized or to go unnoticed and uncomforted. Talk and pray together, thanking God for the love and good times associated with the pet.

Just as there is pain and a time of recuperation with physical wounds, there is pain with emotional wounds—and there must also be a time of recuperation.

It hurts desperately to lose someone you love or something you cherish. When you love deeply, you feel the loss deeply. The loneliness is severe, the pain intense. But God said He would never leave us or forsake us. We may suffer but we don't suffer alone. He is in that valley with us.

WHEN WE FACE DEATH

How do we face death, whether it be our own or the death of a loved one? Our hope is in God. If we have had a foundation of faith laid, if Jesus is Lord of our life, if the Holy Spirit resides within us, when our time of grief comes, we will be able to bear it victoriously.

Several years ago I developed severe complications before the birth of our third child. One night, I was so ill that I literally could not lift my head off the pillow. The room was dark; I was alone. Suddenly the room was flooded with the most glorious light I have ever seen. I saw shining, illuminating, glittering, sparkling crystals of shimmering light; and then came strains of the most beautiful orchestral music I've ever heard.

I felt bathed in God's love. At that moment, without a doubt I thought, "I must be dying;" but there was no fear, only joy and peace. I cannot explain this experience. I only know that it happened, and that I lived with a new awareness of my Lord after that time.

A few months later, the night before our daughter was born, the Lord came to me in a dream. Since I had suffered so many complications, it was really doubtful that the baby would live. There was also much concern over my own well-being. In the dream, the Lord came and took my hands and said, *Betty, peace I give unto you.* I was flooded again with joy, peace, and strength. What a glorious experience! It is as vivid today as it was sixteen years ago. I praise God for this vision.

The next morning, our baby girl arrived healthy and normal in every way—truly a miracle from God. When I shared the dream with my doctor, tears came to his eyes, and he said, "Betty, that explains it. You had a smile on your face all during the Caesarean section."

Was I close to dying? I don't know. Did I almost lose the baby? I don't know that either. The only thing I do know is that during two different times, once when I thought I was dying and another time when our baby wasn't expected to live, God came in a supernatural way to comfort me. He gave me strength, comfort, and grace when I didn't know what the outcome would be.

I have never lost a child or a husband. But from many of the people with whom I have prayed, I have heard them say: "God gave me the strength." "His strength was sufficient." "He walked through the valley with me." "I didn't think I would survive, but He saw me through."

The night Ed's father died, Ed felt a presence in our bedroom awaken him. He saw his father standing there, saying, "Everything is all right." Later, Ed learned from his sister that this was the exact time his dad had died. (The mention of this experience in no way implies that we condone any attempt to communicate with the dead. This practice is expressly forbidden in Scripture; see Lev. 19:31). Ed believes that it was God's way of letting him know that his father was on his way home, and that God allowed him to stop off and say good-bye.

WHERE THERE IS LIFE, THERE IS HOPE

Those who die knowing Jesus have just gone on ahead of us to be with Him. They are free from all pain, and we each have that same glorious promise of life eternal.

I don't want to instill false hope in the families of those who died without openly accepting Jesus; but on the other hand, when loved ones die, you may not know what their last thoughts were.

In that last breath, they may have cried out to Jesus. Even when we think someone is unconscious, we should still pray with him and ask him to accept Jesus. People who have been in a coma, or who were supposedly dying, have later said that they could hear everything around them. We can never know for certain that a person has not accepted Jesus.

If you have a loved one in a coma, be obedient and share Jesus, *whatever* the state of the patient. If there has been a broken relationship, seek to mend it with love and forgiveness. Don't hesitate, don't delay; do it quickly. Strive for reconciliation. Do your part, then leave it in God's hands.

A dear friend, the wife of a Christian psychologist, called to say that her father was critically ill in the hospital.

"I really don't expect him to live," she said.

"Is he a Christian?" I asked.

"You know, I'm really not sure," she responded. "I was discussing this with someone else, and they felt that I shouldn't talk to him about religion since he is so sick."

My heart jumped into my throat. "Oh, don't delay," I said. "Go quickly and share Jesus." I was only confirming what she had already decided.

When she and her husband arrived at the hospital, her dad was in a coma. As she looked down at him, the thoughts flashed through her mind, "You haven't been a dad to me. You were an alcoholic. You didn't give me the love I needed." But as she placed her hand on his shoulder she said, for the first time, "Dad, I love you."

Later, as she and her husband were visiting our

home, she said, "Betty, he actually opened his eyes when I said that. I asked, 'Dad, do you know Jesus as your personal Savior?' And he shook his head no. Then I asked, 'Would you like to know Him?'

" 'Yes,' was his answer."

She asked him to repeat these words after her, and in a halting voice he responded, "Lord Jesus, forgive my sins. Come into my heart as my Savior." When she said "I love you," which was a form of forgiveness, and when he accepted God's forgiveness, the healing power of our Lord began to flow through him. Before they left that night, he was sitting up in bed.

Isn't God wonderful? That dad is now out of the hospital and in a nursing home.

GIVE YOUR GRIEF TO JESUS

Have you suffered a loss? Are you in the depths of grief right now? Tell God how you're aching and that you're lonely, and ask Him to fill the void. God has not forsaken you. He cares; He loves you. Talk to Him and tell Him that your heart is breaking. Pour out your heart, your anguish to Him. If you are angry at God, tell Him that, too. We can be completely honest with Him. Ask Him to take away your bitterness and anger. In some cases, you may even have to say, "God, I forgive You." We must not harbor an unforgiving spirit toward anyone, especially toward God. We must confess it and ask His forgiveness. He does understand. It may be hard to pray. It may be even harder to read the Bible, but those are the two things that will help you come out of the valley of grief.

Allow Jesus to gently cleanse that deep, gaping

wound, to take out all the slivers of resentment, guilt, unforgiveness, self-pity, anger, depression, and fear. Let Him apply His precious healing ointment. Allow Him to heal all the painful memories. Ask Him to bring to your mind all the happy memories of love shared, games played, walks taken, or joys exchanged, and let these precious memories fill the void. ". . . weeping may endure for a night, but joy cometh in the morning" (Ps. 30:5 KJV). My prayer is that joy for you will come in the morning.

BE POSITIVE, BUT BE PREPARED

I had a phone call recently from a Spirit-filled wife who was having a difficult time after she had lost her husband to cancer.

She said, "Betty, we believed with all our hearts that God was going to heal him. We were positive with our confession, and we listened to tapes on healing. In fact, he went to sleep at night listening to tapes. He praised God . . . we just *knew* he was going to be healed.

"But, he died!" And her voice broke in sobs.

She was grieving and she had a heart full of questions. Why, God, why?

Adding to the tragedy was the fact that her husband had not discussed business affairs with her. Overnight she was left with a business that she did not have the vaguest idea of how to manage.

It is not being negative to use good business sense and discuss the possibility of death.

Husbands, discuss business affairs with your wife. Have an up-to-date will. Have all your papers in order where they can be easily found.

Again I say, it is not being negative to be prepared. In fact, how much more positive can one be than to approach life sensibly?

This wife, whose Spirit-filled husband loved her tremendously, I'm sure would be the first to say, "Be positive, but be prepared."

Death is never easy. No one can ever be completely prepared—ever. However, it is not a lack of faith or trust in Him to have our personal and business affairs in order.

The Holy Spirit is not the author of confusion. Our walk out of the valley hand in hand with Jesus is made a little easier when each step is taken in His divine order.

GOD, I REALLY DO TRUST YOU

You have gone *through* the valley when you are able to accept your agonizing loss. When you finally arrive at that place where you can partially resume your old pattern of life, when the wound is healed to a point that you believe you will be able to make a new life for yourself, then you can pick up the pieces of your shattered life and go on.

There is a beautiful truth found in the Twenty-third Psalm. David wrote, "Yea, though I walk through the valley of the shadow of death . . ." (v. 4 kjv). What a comfort it is to know God won't leave us in the valley, but He'll walk through the valley with us.

In *Overcoming Anxiety,* Gerald Schomp wrote: "For the Christian, death is just another of the momentous transformations that occur throughout life. As always, we must lose something in order to gain something greater. We grow up and leave the family in order to live with one we love enough to marry. As we lose the things of this imperfect world, we gain the perfection of the next . . . As profitable an arrangement as we could ever hope for."*

A PRAYER FOR THE GRIEF-STRICKEN
(Make this your own personal prayer.)

"Lord, I don't always understand Your timetable or Your ways, but I know You have every one of our days numbered. I do know that not one thing comes our way without Your knowledge.

"But God, my heart is breaking from grief. Please, Lord, set me free from this grief, this loneliness and sorrow. Set me free from bitterness, self-pity, anger, and depression. Take away the hopelessness and despair.

"Lord, I release my loved one to You. Thank You for forgiving me if there were things I left undone. Help me to forgive myself. Take away any guilt I have. And God, I must confess that at times I've doubted Your love. I've felt anger and unforgiveness toward You. Please forgive me. Let me feel Your love and forgiveness in a special way right now.

"Jesus, walk back with me through the times of sickness, the accident, the death and loss, and wipe away all the panic, the horror, the hopelessness and

---

Overcoming Anxiety by Gerald Schomp (Cincinnati: Messenger Press, 1976), p. 112. Used by permission.

despair. Lord, cleanse those deep wounds and heal my painful memories.

"Lord, heal me; bind up my wounds, heal my broken heart, help me to pick up the pieces of my life. God, change my mourning to joy, fill the aching void in my life with Your love. Heal me in spirit, soul, and body. Walk with me out of this valley of sorrow.

"Thank You, Father, for I pray in Jesus' name. Amen."

SCRIPTURES ON GRIEF

Psalm 23:4: "Even when walking through the dark valley of death I will not be afraid, for you are close beside me, guarding, guiding all the way."

Psalm 40:1: "I waited patiently for God to help me; then he listened and heard my cry."

Psalm 46:1: "God is our refuge and strength, a tested help in times of trouble."

Psalm 57:1: "O God, have pity, for I am trusting you! I will hide beneath the shadow of your wings until this storm is past."

Psalm 119:28: "I weep with grief; my heart is heavy with sorrow; encourage and cheer me with your words."

Psalm 145:14: "The Lord lifts the fallen and those bent beneath their loads."

Psalm 147:3: "He heals the broken-hearted, binding up their wounds."

Isaiah 53:4 (KJV): "Surely he hath borne our griefs, and carried our sorrows. . . ."

Isaiah 61:1,2: "The Spirit of the Lord God is upon me, because the Lord has anointed me to bring good news to the suffering and afflicted. He has sent me to comfort the broken-hearted, to announce liberty to captives and to open the eyes of the blind. He has sent me to tell those who mourn that the time of God's favor to them has come. . . ."

Isaiah 61:3: "To all who mourn in Israel He will give:
Beauty for ashes;
Joy instead of mourning;
Praise instead of heaviness. . . ."

John 14:18: "I will not abandon you or leave you as orphans in the storm—I will come to you."

Matthew 28:20 (KJV): ". . . and lo, I am with you alway, even unto the end of the world."

2 Timothy 4:17 (KJV): "The Lord stood with me, and strengthened me. . . ."

IV

OUT OF THE VALLEY
OF DEPRESSION

The Spirit of the Lord is upon me . . . he has sent me to heal the brokenhearted and to announce that captives shall be released and the blind shall see, that the downtrodden shall be freed from their oppressors, and that God is ready to give blessings to all who come to him.
—Luke 4:18,19

As you begin reading this chapter on depression, I want to share the glorious news that if you have a family member who is depressed, or if you yourself are depressed, you can be set free. *Jesus will bring you out of your valley of depression.*

David exclaimed in Psalm 30:11,12, "He turned my sorrow into joy! He took away my clothes of mourning and gave me gay and festive garments to rejoice in so that I might sing glad praises to the Lord. . . ." What God did for David, He will do for you.

No one escapes Satan's fiery darts of depression. We've all had times of feeling blue, rejected, or discouraged. For some, these are minor, temporary feelings. For others, they are times that can only be called the "dark night of the soul," with a suffocating feeling of hopelessness and despair. David must have felt the same way when he said, "Save me, O my God. The floods have risen. Deeper and deeper I sink in the mire; the waters rise around me. I have wept until I am exhausted; my throat is dry and hoarse; my eyes are swollen with weeping, waiting for my God to act" (Ps. 69:1-3).

One young Christian mother, in the pit of despair, said that she felt as if she were losing her sanity because wave upon wave of depression, each wave increasingly intense, rolled over her. She had fought a lonely spiritual battle until gradually she turned to fantasy for escape. Life was being drained from her. When she and a friend drove from another state to one of our meetings for prayer, she was so depressed and tense, she was actually nauseated. Later, she wrote, "As you introduced Jesus into each situation of my past that had hurt me, and as you asked Him to break the chains around me, I actually felt the oppression lifting. *God rescued me*."

What a thrill to see this person one year later. Smiling, filled with God's love and peace, she could say as David: "I waited patiently for God to help me; then he listened and heard my cry. He lifted me out of the pit of despair. . . ." (Ps. 40:1,2).

We've asked many audiences, "Is there anyone who has never suffered depression?" We have never found a single one. Depression is one of Satan's mightiest weapons. In no way can a Christian be *possessed*, even though he be in the pit of depression. He is *oppressed*, as we are all oppressed by the enemy from time to time. We've all said at times: "I'm so blue I could die." "Life seems hopeless." "I just give up." Why do we get into these valleys of depression?

CAUSES OF DEPRESSION

There are basically three causes of depression: circumstantial, physical, and spiritual. This is a simplified categorization, of course, for the causes are varied and complex. Occasionally there is no obvious cause for depression; rather *it is an all-out attack from the devil*.

Do remember, however, that whatever the cause of your depression, Jesus can heal you and bring you out of the valley to the mountaintop.

ADVERSE CIRCUMSTANCES CAN CAUSE DEPRESSION

1. When a person loses a loved one in death it is certainly a time of grief and loneliness. Satan will not pass up an opportunity to come against the wounded as they struggle to cope with their devastating loss. He will attempt to infect the wound with depression.

2. The death of a relationship or a broken friendship may bring a despondent feeling. David experienced this also. In Psalm 41:9,10 he said, "Even my best friend has turned against me—a man I completely trusted; how often we ate together. Lord, don't you desert me! . . ." Children often become deeply depressed after their parents are divorced. They grieve and may tend to feel they are to blame.

3. Loss of something cherished causes a wound. Whether the loss is an inheritance, life savings, a home or a job, the wound may fester with futility, resentment, or bitterness. The death of a dream or vision may bring on a feeling of discouragement and hopelessness. Saying good-bye to a husband who is going on an extended tour of service or work duty can

certainly make a wife feel depressed. The loss of love in a marriage can bring a deep, despondent feeling. There may be no divorce, but there are daily reminders that something beautiful is gone.

4. After the children have gone to college or married, there may be long afternoons when the house seems lonely. Parents often have the "empty-nest" feeling. A joyous visit with the grandchildren may later only intensify the sadness and the feeling of being at "loose ends."

5. What we put into our minds can bring on depression: soap operas, trashy novels, gloomy movies. I remember a lady who called in tears saying, "I'm so terribly depressed." To make a long story short, she was addicted to soap operas, and on that day's tear jerker, the leading man had died. She had become so emotionally involved that she reacted as if it were a personal loss. Christians should not spend time watching soap operas or gloomy, sad movies. Too much precious time is wasted on such. The Word admonishes us to *redeem* the time.

6. Many people suffer from holiday depression. Especially is this true of the Christmas season. Suicide Prevention Centers have noted that more people are depressed and suicidal in December and January than at any other time.

7. Ironically, after a big success or accomplished goal, there may be a let-down feeling, a time of lethargy. This happens so frequently after a baby is born, it even has a name: the post-partum blues.

8. Loss of self-worth, self-esteem, or a feeling of uselessness, may bring on depression. This occurs often at retirement, or when a person's reputation is

damaged, or when an expected promotion does not materialize. If the person is not able to praise God for all things, he may feel depressed and say, "Life is over; I might as well give up."

9. Some people tend to be more melancholy than others. The least little thing—a *slight* rejection, the loss of a sale, even hearing a sad song on the radio—can trigger a bout of depression. "This is just the way I am; I'm easily depressed," they say. God's Word says in 2 Corinthians 5:17, "Therefore, if any man be in Christ, he is a new creature: old things are passed away; behold, all things are become new" (KJV). We are new creatures in Jesus; we are to be conformed to His image. We don't have to drag that chain of depression around with us.

10. Desiring so deeply something from God other than what we have can bring on depression: being single but having an overwhelming desire for marriage and children; being in one city but always wanting to be somewhere else; yearning for tremendous success but having only moderate accomplishment or failure. These unfulfilled desires can open the door for the enemy to saturate us with depression.

LIFE OR DEATH IS IN OUR MOUTH

Job said, "The thing which I greatly feared is come upon me . . ." (Job 3:25 KJV). Some people actually place a curse on themselves. Especially is this true if a member of their family is emotionally ill or deeply depressed. The child may live in constant fear that he will become just like his mentally ill parent. Some parents pass on to their children a negative inheritance by saying, "You're moody just like your uncle;" or "You're going to be easily depressed just like your aunt."

It is true. Observations of counselors reveal that depressed parents tend to raise depressed, negative, complaining children. It is also true that we have death and life in our tongue (see Prov. 18:21 KJV).

A person I know whose relative had spent her life in a mental institution always feared that she, too, would someday end up in a psychiatric hospital. Such an individual may set into motion a "self-fulfilling prophecy." If this person keeps her eyes on herself, her problem, or her past, before long she *may* be depressed—just as she feared.

K'S STORY

"We are pressed on every side by troubles, but not crushed and broken. We are perplexed because we don't know why things happen as they do, but we don't give up and quit . . .(2 Cor. 4:18).

If we are honest and face reality, many people *do* live in depressing situations. They have all kinds of problems: an alcoholic mate, a child on dope, or a terminally ill parent. They may be in the midst of a financial disaster, or in a situation brought on by an injustice or a crime committed against them. Their only hope of deliverance is Jesus.

The following testimony is from a young Christian mother. She said, "I always thought things like this didn't happen to dedicated Christians." When she was six months pregnant with her second child, her husband left her, with no money, car, or job. He supposedly was a Christian, but he had started drinking shortly after they married. She writes:

I must have gotten him out of jail 100 times in 3½ years. I did everything I knew to do to win him back as a husband and to the Lord, but he rejected us repeatedly. Finally he left and did not return. My divorce was even more painful and traumatic than having cancer, as a 21-year-old girl.

However, with God's help, I managed beautifully for five years in raising my children by myself. Suddenly, a binding power came over my mind. I felt there was no use trying any longer. Some days I'd wake up feeling okay; then some little situation or comment would send me into a black mood.

During this time, I walked around not thinking; my mind seemed cluttered with a maze of black vines. At times, I had trouble carrying on a sensible conversation because I couldn't even think what I was going to say. I became afraid of life; I fell behind in my work. I could not sit still; I was nervous. I hid in my home from friends. I couldn't concentrate to read my Bible. I could not pray. I was so lonely.

Finally, I became so depressed I would just sit and go over the details of how I would do away with myself. I was tired of being a mother, daddy, provider, running a business—tired of feeling that no one cared.

That was the state I was in as I drove to your inner healing meeting that night. In fact, I was so confused I became lost driving. I felt as if I were running for my life. The air even felt heavy around me.

But praise the Lord, that is all in the past—because that night just sitting out in a large group of people while you prayed for inner healing, God reached down and instantly and miraculously touched me and healed my mind and body. *All* my symptoms are gone. My mind is clear. Praise His Name!

Not everyone is healed instantly—physically or emotionally. We certainly do not want to give the impression that all the people with whom we prayed were healed on the spot, because they were not.

Healing may be a process; for some, to our human eyes, it may appear that they have not been healed at all. But in this woman's experience that night, *no one* prayed with her individually. Jesus alone touched and healed her. So don't give up!

It's not the circumstances, but how we deal with them, that causes our depression. Corrie ten Boom's life is a good example of not allowing circumstances to overwhelm one. Despite the unbelievable humiliation and torture of a Nazi concentration camp, she overcame hatred and resentment and refused to give in to depression—by the grace of God.

The key to overcoming depression brought on by circumstances is to do as Paul did: ". . . For I have learned, in whatsoever state I am, therewith to be content" (Phil. 4:11 KJV). "Always be joyful. Always keep on praying. No matter what happens, always be thankful, for this is God's will for you who belong to Christ Jesus" (1 Thess. 5:16–18).

PHYSICAL PROBLEMS
CAN CAUSE DEPRESSION

1. Severe physiological problems, such as a brain tumor or a stroke, can cause depression and bring on personality changes. Some medications and treatments for the illness cause mood changes, emotional instability, and depression.

2. Less serious physical problems can cause that "I don't care" feeling. Perhaps you need a physical check-up. You may have low-grade infection, hormone imbalance, or disease. First, go to God in prayer and ask Him to heal you. Ask Him which avenue He wants to use: divine healing (which is supernatural) or natural healing through doctors and medication.

3. A mother staying up night after night with a seriously ill child may hold up with tremendous strength and composure until the crisis is over; then she may "fall apart."

4. Some women use their physiological make-up as a reason for periodically having the blues. There may be a real hormonal problem, but it may also be an excuse to succumb to the blues.

5. Overwork and fatigue can open the door to depression. Too much to do in too short a time can bring on a bout of "I give up; it will never get done." Exhaustion can bring on an emotional overload, resulting in depression. There are consequences when we abuse our bodies through lack of rest.

6. On the other hand, some people need *more* to do. A person who stays in the house constantly and never goes outside to take a walk and breathe in God's fresh air, may easily become depressed. Our bodies must

have exercise. Looking at four walls all day encourages a person toward self-pity and certainly leads to lethargy.

7. Not eating properly is a cause of depression. School personnel have discovered that children who lack proper nutrition tend to do their work more slowly. Their attention span is short; they tend to daydream more frequently and are more irritable. Dieting to the point of practically eliminating food intake may be a reason for feeling "weepy."

8. Liquor and drug addiction are two things noted for destroying the body not only physically but also emotionally. Many alcoholics are chronically depressed people.

9. People who are scarred or incapacitated from an accident may have to face Satan on the emotional battleground.

C'S STORY

". . . Heal me, for my body is sick, and I am upset and disturbed. My mind is filled with apprehension and with gloom. Oh, restore me soon" (Ps. 6:2,3).

This was the prayer of a young woman who suffered from depression, primarily because of physical problems. Praise the Lord, He did heal her and she is out of her lonely valley. In fact, she and her husband are on the staff of a growing, Spirit-filled church. This is her testimony:

I have had a physical problem for about four years

and have had three operations. Not only did I have physical problems, but spiritual problems as well. One and a half years ago, my husband and I accepted the Lord and heard that Jesus could heal today. But after many prayers over several months, I still wasn't healed. There seemed to be something blocking my healing. Perhaps it was fear, because I had fears of all kinds. I had reached the place where I was even afraid to leave home. I hadn't been to church in weeks.

I felt depressed and confused. One day, when a friend and I were praying, I cried out to God, "Please send someone to help me understand what is going on." I knew that where there was fear, there was no faith. That very day after our prayer a friend called and said, "I want you to talk to Betty Tapscott." Later Betty did pray with me for inner healing. She asked Jesus to heal the memories of when I was so alone and afraid. A very special healing took place that day.

She also prayed for the completion of my physical healing. There was an area in my left shoulder where there was a deep indentation because of the many surgeries. The physical therapist said that this particular area would be very difficult to rebuild, and I just hated even to look in the mirror and see myself. Betty told me to sing and praise God and to look in the mirror and thank God that He made me just the way He did. As I began to praise God for all these things, in five days God performed a creative miracle in my shoulder. He literally filled in that area, and it looks just like the other shoulder. I was seeing it but could hardly believe what a miracle He had done. He had given me an outward sign of what He was doing inside.

The Word of God says to praise Him in ALL things. I was beginning to understand how important praise was. You praise Him not because you feel like it, but because God says to do so.

SPIRITUAL PROBLEMS CAN CAUSE DEPRESSION

Do Christians get depressed? Yes, unfortunately they do, at times. Just being a Christian doesn't mean we will be excluded from Satan's fiery darts and the pressures of life.

Tim LaHaye wrote, ". . . it's not a consequence of 'body chemistry,' 'other people,' or 'the pressures of life'; but our own mental attitude toward those pressures which induces depression. . . . Depression-prone people should scrutinize their thought process to see if they are controlled by Jesus."*

The following are some of the spiritual causes of depression:

1. Drifting from the Lord, not attending church services or not being in Spirit-led fellowships can cause an empty, depressed feeling.

2. If you have known the fullness of the Lord and are not praying in the Spirit, there may be a feeling of *unrest*. There may be a hunger that only fellowship and communion with God can fill.

How to Win Over Depression by Tim LaHaye (Grand Rapids, Michigan: Zondervan, 1974), p. 192. Used by permission.

3. Depression may come from lack of spiritual food. We feed the body spiritually by reading God's Word. David had this to say about God's Word: "I weep with grief; my heart is heavy with sorrow; encourage and cheer me with your words" (Ps. 119:28).

4. Negative speech can bring on depression. Not praising God in all circumstances will allow Satan to fill our thoughts and mouth with negative confession. We must "Always give thanks for everything to our God and Father in the name of our Lord Jesus Christ" (Eph. 5:20).

5. Unforgiveness can block God's healing power. When our minds become poisoned with resentment, bitterness, anger, and self-pity, the result may be depression. Lying awake at night or brooding during the day, going over some past hurt and wondering, "How can I get even?" will cause a person to sink into a pit of despair. We must forgive others, and we must also forgive ourselves.

6. Seeking information from any source other than God will bring on depression. LaHaye says:

> I have seen enough to convince me that all depression is not the result of demon possession or oppression, but all contact with demons or evil spirits produces depression. An individual may consult mystics, ouija boards, knocking tables, tea leaves, or readers or palmists in any major city, but almost invariably within a few hours or possibly days he will be engulfed by a spirit of depression.*

7. Guilt, whether it is real or false, may bring on

*Ibid., p. 181.

depression. Unresolved guilt can be devastating. A young college student had suffered a nervous breakdown and had been in a psychiatric hospital for six months when her husband brought her for inner healing. This young woman was from a family who loved her dearly. She had a delightful personality and was beautiful. She had a sparkle about her and a deep love for Jesus; yet, Satan had come against her and overwhelmed her with depression. The root causes were guilt and perfectionism. She poured out her frustrations and feelings of failure over not being able to do everything perfectly, and her feeling of guilt over past sins. We prayed for inner healing, binding Satan in the name of Jesus and taking authority over the giants that had come against her. Then we prayed for healing of memories.

The Lord broke the chains of guilt, perfectionism, and depression. In three weeks' time, she was dismissed from the hospital and sent home. Her letters are proof that she continues to rest in the Lord and His promise that there is no condemnation in Jesus. She is not completely whole yet, but she is on her way.

8. God calls people to fast and when He does so, it can be a wonderful, enriching experience. But a body weakened physically by lack of food can bring on depression. We have counseled depressed people who were fasting, and we have found that it was obviously not the Lord who told them to stop eating entirely.

L'S STORY

"But O my soul, don't be discouraged. Don't be upset. Expect God to act! For I know that I shall again have plenty of reason to praise him for all that he will do. He is my help! He is my God!" (Ps. 42:11).

Several years ago a man brought his wife to us for inner healing. They were dedicated Christians, and had been busy serving the Lord, sharing their testimonies with many groups of people, when she went into a deep depression.

There had been an emotional problem and resistance to the husband's authority. He was a new Christian. The wife knew that her rebellion and resentment had to go, so she started fasting. She stopped taking some prescribed medication and started staying up at night reading her Bible. The combination of no rest, lack of food, and stopping her medication gave Satan a chance to really come against her—and come against her he did! He had just been waiting to get his foot in the door, because their testimony had blessed so many people.

The outcome of his all-out attack was a depression so severe that she was unable to talk or walk. She could not eat or take care of her body. When her husband brought her to us, she was in a catatonic state; saliva drooled down her chin. We had met this couple previously, and the love we had for them deepened as we saw how Satan had tried to devour her.

Later, she shared the feelings she experienced that day during our prayer for inner healing:

Betty, the thing that I felt more than anything was your love. I knew you *loved* me. It was not pity. You said, "I know you must feel embarrassment and self-consciousness;" and oh, I did. You were the first one to voice what I felt but could not say! You held my hand. Ed touched my arm, and Betty, you kept saying, "I love you, and God loves you." You and Ed prayed for me for inner healing. I could not repeat after you, but you said to repeat silently, and I thought, "Oh, she understands. She knows that I want to talk, but can't."

One by one, you had me repeat silently after you, binding all the negative forces attacking me. I remember the Holy Spirit seemed to speak to you, Betty, about a particular area. You left the room and asked my husband a question or two. His answers confirmed what the Holy Spirit had said to you. There had been a deep hurt in my past, a wound buried so deeply in my subconscious that I had blotted it from my conscious mind. Tenderly you said, "Oh, Jesus, go back to the time of this hurt, this injustice, and cleanse and heal. Lord, help her forgive."

You told me later that as you asked me to forgive, a tiny tear came to my eye, and that this was the only outward sign of anything taking place on the inside during the entire time I was there.

You continued the prayer for healing of memories. At one point, Betty, you showed such an overpowering love and compassion for me when you tenderly touched my forehead and said, "Oh, Jesus, touch her, touch her, Jesus, and heal her." Ed then prayed and asked the Lord to heal a glandular problem that I had, and the Lord did heal it.

As you were praying and talking, God kept bring-ing things to my mind that I didn't realize were there. God completely erased the pain of the past.

There was a lot of guilt and unforgiveness. I was in spiritual warfare, and at times, I felt as if my spirit and my physical body were disconnected.

My mind whirled and whirled, faster and faster. When someone talked negatively to me, I felt so cold, as if I were about to die. But when God's saints prayed for me and touched me, I felt warmth and His love.

As you and Ed were being led of the Spirit that day and as you prayed, God healed. I was coming out of bondage. You prayed for specific things as the Lord revealed them to you.

I don't know how to describe it, but He "re-grouped" me. I had been falling apart; I felt as if I were dying. But God touched me and filled me with His love. I felt warmth. He renewed my mind. God showed me I had all these roots in my life that needed to go, and He clipped them off. He clipped off the confusion, guilt, unforgiveness, rebellion, pride. He healed it all.

I didn't realize I had all those hurts and painful memories buried deep inside. I had a negative reac-tion towards men, but God healed that also. My husband is now the spiritual head of our household.

I've always had a hard time receiving love, but praise God, you and Ed ministered with love. It was your ministry that pulled out that old deep root of depression. God didn't even leave a scar.

That night after we prayed, her husband had to

carry "L" back to the car to begin the long journey back to their home state. There was not one visible sign that she had been healed, but Ed and I knew that God had touched her. And indeed, a few days later, she got up out of bed, walked to where her husband was, and started speaking. Her inner healing had come forth. She was out of the valley.

A year later I was speaking in this woman's home state when a beautiful prophecy was given. To my delight it was this lady—now whole and normal in every way—who voiced God's Word to that group.

When I was interviewing her for this testimony she said, "The *way* you ministered brought healing also. So, Betty, please tell people when they minister to:

1. *Touch people as they pray.* You and Ed held my hand and touched my arm as you prayed.

2. *Show love—not pity, but love.* I could feel your love and compassion.

3. *Quote Scriptures.* Oh, how the Word fed my spirit. It ministered life to me.

4. *Minister in gentleness.* One lady came to pray for me and because I had taught the faith message, she said, 'Now, you just get ahold of yourself. Put your will in motion. Just make an effort.' I wanted to scream, 'I can't! Can't you see? I can't!'

5. *Never stop praying and don't give up.* I was so afraid you and Ed would give up on me because I knew I could not utter one word. But you didn't.

6. *Don't go by what you see, but by what the Spirit says.* "You said to my husband and me as we were leaving, 'We know God has healed you, even though we don't see any difference.'" (We were not "claiming" her

healing. The Lord gave us a direct word that He had touched her.)

This lady was one of the most depressed persons I've ever seen, but Jesus set her free and healed her. He loves each of us the same way.

STEPS OUT OF THE VALLEY OF DEPRESSION

1. Do you have a personal relationship with Jesus? If not, by all means ask forgiveness of your sins and invite Jesus into your heart. Jesus is your only way to peace. Spend time in prayerful meditation. "He will keep in perfect peace all those who trust in him, whose thoughts turn often to the Lord" (Is. 26:3).

2. Get into a loving Christian fellowship that praises and worships Jesus. Don't try to carry your burdens by yourself. God wants you to give those burdens to Him, and He has others standing by who want to help you.

3. Read your Bible every day. Make Scripture cards with God's promises on them and place them all around the house. Memorize and quote God's promises. Saturate yourself with the Word.

4. Have someone pray with you to be set free from any negative spirit coming against you. God's Word says, ". . . whatever you bind on earth is bound in heaven, and whatever you free on earth will be freed in heaven" (Matt. 18:18).

5. Praise God whether you feel like it or not. First Thessalonians 5:16–18 says, "Always be joyful. Always keep on praying. No matter what happens, always be thankful, for this is God's will for you who belong to Christ Jesus." Make a list of all the things for which you

can thank Him: Can you see? Can you hear? Can you walk? Do you have food to eat? As the song goes:

> Count your blessings,
> Name them one by one,
> And it will surprise you
> What the Lord has done.

6. Fill your house and car with joyous praise music. Get in the habit of singing as you work. When I am tired, I sing the Scripture song, "The Joy of the Lord Is My Strength." I can feel His strength and joy flooding me as I praise Him.

7. Practice proper temple maintenance. "Know ye not that your body is the temple of the Holy Ghost . . ." (1 Cor. 6:19 KJV). Eat nutritious food. Leave off the junk food, especially excess coffee and soft drinks. Get plenty of rest and sleep. Get the proper amount of exercise.

8. If your depression is caused by exhaustion and too many jobs to do, start eliminating some of the tasks. Don't overload your emotional circuit. Back away from some of the stress and pressure.

9. If the devil has you feeling sorry for yourself, tell him you are not going to have a "pity party" and demand that he leave you alone. Then, *do something for someone else.* Gloom has a way of vanishing when we think of those with problems bigger than our own. While in the midst of your "blues," send a card to cheer a friend; take someone a joy gift, or visit someone in the hospital. Most important, pray for others.

10. Live in the present. Forget the past and look forward to what lies ahead (see Phil. 3:13). Don't spend your time thinking how you were mistreated or how

you would like to get even. Don't worry about the future. Life is short. Live just one day at a time. If one day gets too burdensome for you, say, "God help me get through this morning or even this hour." Thank Him when He does. Step by step He will walk through your valley of depression with you.

11. Fill your days with worthwhile activities. Do something constructive with your life. Join a Bible study group, prayer group, or hospital volunteers. However, don't over-do. There must be a balance. The main thing is don't sit at home and vegetate! Get out of the house, and do something that blesses someone else.

12. If you've done everything you know to do and depression still hangs over your head like a cloud, you may need a physical examination. If, after a medical check-up, there is no physical problem, then, by all means, seek out a Christian psychologist, psychiatrist, or counselor. Make certain he is a Christian, however. A non-Christian counselor who scoffs at God, Christianity, or who encourages you to "do your own thing" will only create more problems.

13. Constantly forgive. Whatever the hurt or insult, don't let resentment or anger or self-pity stay in the wound. Practice instant forgiveness. When a painful memory comes to your mind, replace it with a pleasant memory. Use your will to forgive or say, "God, I give you my will; forgive through me."

14. Use the spiritual authority you have through the shed blood of Jesus Christ to fight Satan's attacks. "So use every piece of God's armor to resist the enemy whenever he attacks, and when it is all over, you will still be standing up" (Eph. 6:13).

15. Practice holy living. Turn your back on those practices, thoughts, and activities that are not pleasing to God and that do not glorify Him. Spiritual darkness breeds depression: ". . . As he thinketh in his heart, so is he . . ." (Prov. 23:7 KJV).

16. We must take our eyes off the problem and put our eyes on Jesus. In our own strength we may not be able to cope, but God's Word says ". . . My grace is sufficient for thee: for my strength is made perfect in weakness . . ." (2 Cor. 12:9 KJV). Praise God that "he giveth power to the faint; and to them that have no might he increaseth strength" (Is. 40:29 KJV).

There may be times however, when life becomes heavy and burdensome, and a dark cloud drifts overhead.

Unfortunately, when Christians become depressed, they often find themselves in the net of "What will others think if they know I'm discouraged?" It's a sad state of affairs when a wounded person cannot share his discouragement for fear of being reprimanded for lack of faith or not confessing positively.

Jeremiah 6:14 says, "You can't heal a wound by saying it's not there! . . ." We must remember to respond in love and compassion to those who are emotionally under the weather. We must encourage them to believe that this too shall pass.

PRAYER FOR THE DEPRESSED
(Make this your own personal prayer.)

"Dear Lord, sometimes I'm so depressed I can't even pray. Please set me free from this bondage. I thank

You, Lord, for Your delivering power, and I bind the evil one from me in the mighty name of Jesus. Spirits of depression, anger, fear, self-pity, oppression, guilt, unforgiveness, and any other negative force that has come against me, you are bound and cast out in the name of Jesus. Lord, break all the chains that have bound me.

"Jesus, I pray You will go back to the moment this depression came against me, and set me free from the root cause. Heal all my painful memories. Fill me with Your love, Your peace, and Your joy. I pray You will restore to me the joy of my salvation. Lord Jesus, let joy bubble forth like a river from way down deep inside. I love You, Jesus; I praise You. Bring to my mind all the things for which I can thank You. Lord, help me to reach up and touch You; to keep my eyes on You and not on the problem. Thank You, Lord, for leading me out of the valley. It is in the name of Jesus I pray. Amen."

SCRIPTURE VERSES ON DEPRESSION

Psalm 40:2,3: "He lifted me out of the pit of despair, out from the bog and the mire, and set my feet on a hard, firm path and steadied me as I walked along. He has given me a new song to sing, of praises to our God. . . ."

Psalm 42:11: ". . . O my soul, don't be discouraged. Don't be upset. Expect God to act! For I know that I shall again have plenty of reason to praise him for all that he will do. He is my help! He is my God!"

OUT OF THE VALLEY OF DEPRESSION

Psalm 9:9: "All who are oppressed may come to him. He is a refuge for them in their times of trouble."

Psalm 18:28: "You have turned on my light! The Lord my God has made my darkness turn to light."

Psalm 34:1-3: ". . . I will praise the Lord no matter what happens. I will constantly speak of his glories and grace. I will boast of all his kindness to me. Let all who are discouraged take heart. Let us praise the Lord together, and exalt his name."

Psalm 51:12: "Restore to me again the joy of your salvation, and make me willing to obey you."

Joshua 1:9 KJV: ". . . Be strong and of a good courage; be not afraid, neither be thou dismayed. . . ."

Isaiah 26:3: "He will keep in perfect peace all those who trust in him, whose thoughts turn often to the Lord!"

Isaiah 42:3: "He will not break the bruised reed, nor quench the dimly burning flame. He will encourage the fainthearted, those tempted to despair. . . ."

John 14:27: "I am leaving you with a gift—peace of mind and heart! And the peace I give isn't fragile like the peace the world gives. So don't be troubled or afraid."

2 Corinthians 4:8: "We are pressed on every side by

troubles, but not crushed and broken. We are perplexed because we don't know why things happen as they do, but we don't give up and quit."

Philippians 4:7: ". . . His peace will keep your thoughts and your hearts quiet and at rest as you trust in Christ Jesus."

Colossians 1:13,14: "For he has rescued us out of the darkness and gloom of Satan's kingdom and brought us into the kingdom of his dear Son, who bought our freedom with his blood and forgave us all our sins."

Psalm 69:15,16: ". . . Save me from the pit that threatens me. O Jehovah, answer my prayers, for your loving kindness is wonderful; your mercy is so plentiful, so tender and so kind."

Psalm 6:2,3: ". . . Heal me, for my body is sick, and I am upset and disturbed. My mind is filled with apprehension and with gloom. Oh, restore me soon."

V

DON'T LOSE HOPE

He forgives all my sins. He heals me. He ransoms me from hell. He surrounds me with lovingkindness and tender mercies. He fills my life with good things! My youth is renewed like the eagle's.

—Psalm 103:3–5

There are certain events and people that stand out in your mind. The following testimonies are from people whom the Lord beautifully and gloriously led out of the valley. If He did it for them, He can do it for you!

PAULINE'S STORY*

The stranger's voice on the telephone did not betray her deep inner turmoil. The lady simply gave her name and said, "Please, may I come and see you? I'm so depressed! Will you help me?"

I explained that I was trying to get a new book to the

---

*This story appeared in *Charisma* Magazine, April, 1979. I thank them for allowing me to publish it again in this book. I include this story especially for those who are unfamiliar with the process of inner healing.

publisher by a deadline. "But what is the problem?" I inquired.

With a deep sigh, she replied, "Life is hopeless; I can't go on. I just want to die." Sometimes the person truly believes such statements; sometimes he does not. But always it is a cry for help—and we listen. While I was listening to her, I was also listening to the Holy Spirit; and *He* said, *She means business. See her now!* So I put the manuscript aside and told her she could come to the office.

Pauline arrived after a brief time. She was an attractive Jewish lady, forty-ish. After thanking me for seeing her, she immediately began to share her tragic story—a story of a lifetime of rejection and depression.

Even before she was born, she was unwanted; her mother had tried to abort her. Her father deserted the family when she was two. When her mother remarried, they moved to a small town where they were the only Jewish family. She was constantly ostracized and rejected. At fifteen, she left home and later worked her way through college. She married a lawyer, but her husband's goal in life was to make money. This meant that very little time was left for her or the family.

Her child was autistic; his behavior was not socially acceptable. Consequently, she felt even more rejection and frustration, embarrassment and loneliness. On and on she poured out her hurt and disappointment, her feelings of failure and despair. Eventually, her first marriage ended in divorce. Her second marriage proved to be a disastrous mistake, leaving her an utterly dejected and broken individual, feeling unwanted and unloved by everyone.

Gently, I said, "Pauline, only Jesus can heal your broken and wounded spirit. But He is more interested in healing you spiritually than in any other way." Together we read the Scripture in 1 John 1:9, "But if we confess our sins to him, he can be depended on to forgive us and to cleanse us from every wrong." I shared the plan of salvation and how Jesus had died on the cross for her sins.

At that moment, the Holy Spirit touched Pauline's heart. She responded, "Oh, I do want Jesus. I want to know that I'm forgiven and will have life eternal." With deep repentance, she asked forgiveness and invited Jesus into her heart as her personal Lord and Savior. Thus, the healing process was begun.

"Pauline, what you need now," I said, "is prayer for inner healing."

"What is that?" she asked.

I explained, "Inner healing is the healing of the inner man: the painful memories and emotional wounds. It is the renewing of your mind" (see Rom. 12:2 KJV). "What you've just experienced— salvation—is the greatest healing of all; but God also wants to heal you emotionally and physically. Isaiah 53:5 says, 'He was wounded and bruised for *our* sins. He was chastised that we might have peace; he was lashed—and we were healed!' God wants to heal you: spirit, soul, and body."

Inner healing is not just a psychological experience; it is also a spiritual process based on God's Word, which tells us in Luke 4:18,19 that Jesus was sent to heal the brokenhearted and to announce that captives shall be released.

Inner healing is the process through prayer whereby a person is set free from negative emotions such as fear, rejection, resentment, guilt, unforgiveness, and depression. It is *not* digging up garbage, but throwing away the garbage that's there. It is *not* erasing the memory, but asking Jesus to remove the sting, to anesthetize the pain connected with the memory. It is allowing Jesus to cleanse the wound and remove any splinters of hatred, bitterness, or self-pity lodged in the wound.

Our minds are like computers, filing away every memory in our subconscious. Psychologists tell us that everything that happens to us plays a part in causing us to act or react the way we do. There are many people who live in the past, going over past hurts and disappointments, hanging on to old grudges. They become martyrs to the past. God's Word says to forget the past and look forward to what lies ahead (see Phil. 3:13).

There are other people, however, who wear smiling masks, saying, "Everything is fine," when in fact, they have been deeply wounded emotionally. Jeremiah 6:14 says, "You can't heal a wound by saying it's not there! . . ."

I believe everyone needs inner healing to some degree. To live is to hurt and be hurt, to disappoint and to be disappointed. No one escapes pain in this life. For some, there are only emotional sore spots, tiny bruised places, minor embarrassments. But for others, the wounds are agonizingly deep and painful, the depression immobilizing, and the fears crippling.

Jeremiah 4:4 instructs us to cleanse our minds and hearts, not just our bodies. Inner healing allows Jesus to shine His divine light into all the dark places of our souls and to cleanse and heal.

I continued my explanation of inner healing. "In a way it is a spiritual surgery, allowing Jesus to cut away the growths of inferiority, unworthiness, condemnation, and inadequacy so that we can become the Spirit-filled person God created us to be.

"We forget, it seems, that we are in spiritual warfare and that it is the evil one who sends fear, confusion, and anxiety against us. '. . . God hath not given us the spirit of fear; but of power, and of love, and of a sound mind' (2 Tim. 1:7 KJV). Of course we don't look for an evil spirit under every bush or behind every sneeze. We keep our eyes on Jesus. However, many people allow Satan to walk all over them. I cannot stress enough that Christians cannot be possessed, but they can certainly be oppressed. Many are emotional cripples living in a web of depression, defeat, and discouragement.

"Some may say, 'I thought emotions of jealousy, self-pity, hate, and anger were just the old sinful nature." But where does sin come from? It certainly doesn't come from God. Those negative emotions are links in the chains that keep us in bondage.

"The Good News is that '. . . God will break the chains that bind his people and the whip that scourges them . . .' [Is. 9:4]."

Pauline interrupted me. "This sounds great, but how, just *how* will God set me free? How does He break those chains?"

"There are two steps to inner healing," I replied. "The first is binding Satan and taking authority over the spiritual giants in the name of Jesus. The second step is asking Jesus to heal painful memories and to fill the void in your life.

"There is a prerequisite to inner healing, however, and that is complete forgiveness. We must not, we cannot, continually place blame on those who have hurt us. The whole world is hurting. The evil one is seeking to destroy, devour, and deceive through unforgiveness. Our responsibility is to forgive, to replace our negative emotions with positive ones, and to invite Jesus into each situation. And Jesus Christ introduced into the situation brings healing.

"Matthew 6:14,15 says, 'Your heavenly Father will forgive you if you forgive those who sin against you; but if *you* refuse to forgive *them, he* will not forgive *you*.' We must accept God's forgiveness for our sins, forgive others, and forgive ourselves."

I could see the pensive look that came over Pauline's face as she recalled all the people who had hurt her, but she quickly said, "Oh, I want to forgive. I really do."

So one by one, she lifted each person to the Lord and said, "Lord, I forgive my mother who did not want me, my dad who deserted us. I forgive my stepfather. I forgive the neighbors who ostracized me, the playmates who excluded me, the teachers who embarrassed me. Lord, I forgive my husband and the other woman. I forgive the minister who did not portray Jesus." And her voice broke when she haltingly said, "God, I forgive You for allowing my son to be autistic." And then she added pleadingly, "Please forgive me for blaming You."

When she finished forgiving each person, we then asked Jesus to set her free from every negative force. We claimed God's promise in Matthew 18:18, ". . . whatever you bind on earth is bound in heaven, and whatever you free on earth will be freed in heaven." We had her renounce each spiritual giant that was binding her.

Quietly, but with the authority we have in Jesus, as the Holy Spirit brought each negative force to my mind, I had her repeat, "Spirit of fear, out in the name of Jesus; spirit of depression, out in the name of Jesus." "So if the Son sets you free, you will indeed be free" (John 8:36).

"Pauline," I explained, "since 'Jesus Christ is the same yesterday, today, and forever' [Heb. 13:8], He can heal hurts just the way He can forgive sins." We then continued in the time of ministry by asking Jesus to heal every painful memory. We asked Him to go back to the time of birth and heal the hurt of not being wanted. We prayed that Jesus would heal every traumatic experience. We asked Him to walk through every second of her life and to heal her broken heart and wounded spirit. (See Ps. 147:3).

God did a mighty work as He beamed divine light into the dark areas and healed her inner being. That afternoon, He truly renewed her mind. She threw her arms around me and said, "Oh, I've never felt so happy, so free, so loved. All the depression is gone; all my doubts are gone. Oh, praise the Lord!"

Then her voice became sober. Hesitantly, she said, "Let me tell you what I had planned to do. A few days ago, I sent a copy of my will to a child in another state.

Yesterday I gave another copy to a neighbor. I haven't eaten in two days. In my purse is a bottle of pills. This very day I was going to take the pills and drive my car off a freeway overpass. Today I was going to kill myself."

It took a moment for the impact of what she was saying to hit me. Then with a heart of thanksgiving, I said, "Oh, thank You, Holy Spirit, that I listened to Your voice. Thank You, Lord Jesus, for setting her free and for healing her."

"Remember," I said, as Pauline pulled on her coat and walked to the door, "God loves you; He cares; He's concerned, and He wants you to be completely free and to *stay* free. Don't ever forget that you're special and precious to Him." As I gave her a hug, I added, "Remember, I love you, too."

Just the way God loves Pauline, He loves you and wants to set you free and heal whatever hurt you have. He has a gift for you also, peace of mind and heart (see John 14:27).

P'S STORY

"Come quickly, Lord, and answer me, for my depression deepens; don't turn away from me or I shall die. Let me see your kindness to me in the morning . . ." (Ps. 143:7,8).

One man in the throes of depression walked through the valley for two years before he was healed. Healing is a process and God works in many different ways. Here is the man's story:

I had a good dose of depression with a whole

bunch of problems: loss of self-esteem and no sense of worth. I was an engineer, a good one. My job was my survival, my worth, and when I was laid off unexpectedly, it was a big blow.

It took quite a while to find another job because I was overbearing. I had personality clashes with other people. I did finally land a job, but I had to take a pay cut which made me feel as though I wasn't worth as much as I had been.

When I lost that job, and the next, I really felt worthless. I had given up on God. I reasoned that there couldn't be a God or I wouldn't be feeling like this. One time I cried out, "God, if You're really there, do something!"

By this time, I had gone to physicians and six or eight psychiatrists, looking for help, but I became disenchanted. I would feel better for a few days, but that was mainly from excitement over something new. Then my same old problems would return. I heard of a new medicine and took sick leave from work to be admitted to the hospital for this new treatment. I had an allergic reaction to the medicine and was in a coma for three days. When I was released from the hospital, my wife watched me like a hawk, never leaving me alone. She took me everywhere with her, even to her prayer groups. I would sit there thinking about how I wanted to go home and slash my arteries.

My wife was a tower of faith and saw me through that time. She read several books, one of which was Betty's book, *Inner Healing*. She called her and was able to set up an appointment for us to come and counsel with them. During the appointment, I wasn't too aware of what was happening, due to all my medication. They went through the prayer for the healing of memories, asking the Lord to heal all my hurts and set me free from the spirit of depression.

They suggested that we attend a certain Catholic church. We went to the service and I heard everyone singing, but I didn't want to be around all those happy people. One night we broke into groups of five or six and prayed for one another. I had been so depressed, always looking *inward*. I needed to look out and see others. There was a lady in my group with bandages on her feet. The only family member she had left was a son who had just left her all alone. I realized that others had problems, too. I looked *outward* to others for the first time.

I wanted a demonstrative, "lights and thunder" healing, but it didn't come that way. I cried all the way home that night. The next morning when I woke up, I said to myself, "Maybe I'll live," and that was the beginning of my healing, which is still going on.

We have continued to go to that same Catholic church for their prayer meetings, and I have given my testimony there several times. Once, the leader of the meeting introduced me as the most depressed person he had ever seen.

If you're depressed, start looking out and seeing other people. When you start looking out, then you will look up. And when you look up, you'll see what the Lord wants you to see—the cross in daily life. But the Lord is the one who helps you carry it. Don't give up hope! God is a God of miracles.

DON'T LOSE HOPE

S'S STORY

"He lifted me out of the pit of despair, out from the bog and the mire, and set my feet on a hard, firm path and steadied me as I walked along. He has given me a new song to sing, of praises to our God . . ." (Ps. 40:2,3).

It seemed as if all my life had been spent behind a mask: smiling on the outside, lonely and hurting on the inside, paralyzed with fears, wanting to reach out, but not knowing how. I had fought depression all my life, wondering why I could not be happy. I have a wonderful husband and three gorgeous children who love me and whom I love dearly, a beautiful home, success—everything anyone could possibly want. Yet I was empty on the inside.

About eight years ago, I went to my family doctor seeking help for depression, and I was told that I have a chemical imbalance in my body which causes depression. He prescribed a new drug, an antidepressant. I was told I'd have to take the pills for the rest of my life. Well, they did keep my moods level, and I felt so much better that I called them my happy pills.

But drugs couldn't get to the root of the problem; they just covered it up. The antidepressant led to more prescribed drugs: tranquilizers. First, they were just to help me sleep, and then more and more to fight the anxiety of daily trials and problems. After several years, these weren't enough, so I added a little alcohol, and then more and more. All of these changes occurred so gradually that I never realized I had a problem with the drugs. After all, the doctor had prescribed them.

A year ago, I found the Lord Jesus and was filled with the Holy Spirit, but I was still dependent upon the drugs and alcohol, not realizing even then that I was chemically addicted. I've never ended up drunk in a ditch somewhere; but I began to realize that I needed these things to face life. At this point, I was in the midst of several high-pressure situations. I felt if I could make it through the summer of events, then I would break free from the addictions. The Lord got me through the summer, and then I fell completely apart! I went to bed and could do nothing but cry for days. I hyperventilated, and my heart pounded constantly. I asked, "What are you trying to show me, Lord?" One thing He showed me was that I had abused my body, the temple of His Holy Spirit. I knew without a doubt that I had to quit taking all the medication and stop drinking. During a one-week period, I went to see two doctors, a Christian psychologist, and also to Alcoholics Anonymous. I still didn't find the answer to my deep-seated depression.

Then, one morning, I awoke in sheer panic from a dream that I now believe God sent. I was a little girl again, back in my hometown, running from something, trying to find help, but everywhere I went, the people were demonic figures, laughing at me. No one would help me. I didn't understand what God was trying to show me, but I bound Satan from my thoughts and got out of bed.

Sometime later I went to a Christian bookstore

and picked up a book called *Inner Healing* by Betty Tapscott. I read the book and knew it was the solution to my life-long problem. The Holy Spirit revealed to me that the dream was sent to show me that I had to go back and face the giants, and to forgive the people who had hurt me. As I looked back at my childhood, I began to understand why I had become the way I was. My father had been an alcoholic, and my mother was very bowed down with negatives in her life. So I never received the love I needed as a child. I had to go back and be honest with myself, and not hide or bury hurts behind a mask.

Betty was speaking at a nearby church the following week. She led us gently through inner healing. She helped me go back with Jesus and face rejection, fear of rejection, fear of failure, the spirit of perfectionism, spirit of guilt, fear of speaking in public or calling people on the phone, pride, inferiority, and a spirit of grief that I had buried deep down in me when we lost little twin boys shortly after their birth . . . many more things that I didn't even know I had in me. I couldn't believe I was oppressed with so many spirits! But now I praise the Lord because He stripped the old cracked mask so that the real me could be set free!

Jesus healed all of the hurts, fears, grief, addiction—everything that had me paralyzed spiritually and emotionally. Jesus is the one who made us, so He's really the only one who can mend us when we are broken! He knows everything about us, and He wants us to be whole, inside and outside.

Since this time, even though I was delivered from the addictions, Satan has tried to tempt me to return to the alcohol during times of stress. It was a step-by-step process of trusting Jesus to provide the strength, His strength, to conquer it! And now, I am more than conqueror through Jesus, for I have defeated alcoholism, addiction to drugs, depression, and fear. I'm out of my valley.

M. C.'S STORY

". . . Be strong and of a good courage; be not afraid, neither be thou dismayed . . ." (Josh. 1:9 KJV).

The following testimony came from a lady whose main problem was depression. M. C. shared all her hurts as a child and as an adult: her divorce and the difficulty of rearing a son by herself. She shared also about God's gift of a new Christian husband and precious daughter.

She later described her inner healing this way: "Jesus took a trash basket in one hand and a dust cloth in the other and cleaned house. When He finished, I felt clean and bright on the inside."

After we finished praying for inner healing and asking the Lord to set her free from depression, I felt impressed to pray also for her physical healing.

She writes in her testimony,

I had told Betty I was in perfect health, but actually I had sinus problems something awful. I had infections all the time, my back hurt constantly, and my poor feet—I had undergone three operations. I wore expensive, special braces and had to wear corrective shoes that looked terrible. The doctor had said that I would have to have still another foot operation, and I just said, "Forget it." I walked as little as I could and just put up with the pain.

Betty prayed that God would heal me completely. I said, "Amen," and I stood up. Praise the Lord! I felt as if I'd grown a foot! It felt as if someone had taken my backbone and reconstructed the vertebrae. I didn't feel any pain. What an overpowering feeling of joy!

Later, at Christmastime, I went shopping for two hours in high heels, not corrective shoes, with no pain.

I praise God for my physical and emotional healing. I had such a reading problem as a child that I went to pieces when I had to read aloud. But Betty prayed that Jesus would sit next to me as a little child and tell me how pleased He was. Well, later, when I was in my ladies' Bible study, we had to look up Bible verses. Before I realized it, I had volunteered to read not once, but twice. Then it came to me: "Hey, I'm reading out loud." Now I'm the first to volunteer to read. Praise the Lord!

You know, the main reason I came for prayer was because of depression. I would have periods of depression, sometimes minor and sometimes for days. Well, I have not had any more problems with depression. I wake up cheerful and full of energy.

Not only did God heal me emotionally, but physically as well.

B'S STORY

". . . The Lord my God has made my darkness turn to light" (Ps. 18:28).

After a luncheon for two hundred ladies at an army base, two ladies came for prayer. One of the ladies had undergone many shock treatments for severe depression. There was heaviness and sadness all over her face: a portrait of hopelessness and futility. She had tried to commit suicide more than once. The friend who brought her said, "Many people think it is hopeless, but I know God wants to heal her."

The lady chimed in, "Oh, everyone thinks I'm crazy." She was suffering from satanic oppression, yes, but crazy she was not.

"First of all," I asked, "are you a Christian?"

"Yes," she said, "I am."

"Do you have any physical problems besides this depression?"

"Yes, I do. My back just kills me," she said.

"Have you ever seen God perform a miracle?"

"No, I haven't," she said expectantly.

"Well, God is going to let you see a miracle right now."

And the Lord, true to His Word, healed her back. Praise His name!

Then we prayed, asking the Lord to set her free from her depression. Instantly there was a tremendous change. Her face even looked different. The change was from night to day. She was smiling. She stood up and ran into the main dining room and exclaimed to the surprised waitresses, "God just healed me!"

We have kept in touch. Her letters reveal that all her problems are not solved. In fact, her circumstances at home are horrible; but she is allowing Jesus to carry the load for her.

I recently spoke again in her city, and who do you suppose was one of the officers of this Christian group? My friend! My heart almost burst with joy as I looked at one of God's miracles standing before me.

Her deep faith in God was evidenced by the serenity on her face. I gave her a great big hug and said, "You look just great." She reminded me that it had been three years since God delivered her from depression. I admired a butterfly necklace she was wearing. "That represents your new life in Jesus, doesn't it? You are a new creature."

After the meeting was over and we were having one last prayer with all the officers, I felt her place something in my hand. It was her butterfly necklace. "I want you to have it," she said. That necklace is one of my most prized possessions, a daily reminder that God does heal today—even "impossible" cases.

L'S STORY

"All who are oppressed may come to him. He is a refuge in their times of trouble" (Ps. 9:9).

We were in Canada holding an inner healing service. A lady who had been emotionally wounded came to the meeting. A cloud of heaviness, gloom, and futility hung over her head. She watched as we prayed for the others, and when the last person was leaving, the pastor handed me a note from the lady which read, "May I talk to you?" When I walked over to her, she said, "I don't want you to pray with me, please promise you won't; I just want to talk. Someone prayed with me a year ago, and I cried uncontrollably for one hour. I'm afraid of what I might do again if someone prayed for me." So, I just listened as she shared. She was terribly depressed. She had been labeled a schizophrenic. She poured out her hurts. She doubted that God loved her, that He would heal her.

I encouraged her to rest in the assurance that He did love her very, very much and that He did want her to be whole. The next night she came back to the meeting, and to my surprise she came up for prayer.

"Please, would you pray for me tonight?"

Praise God! He touched her and gently, ever so gently, she was set free from the bondage of depression, confusion, fear, and double-mindedness. God's power went through her, and Jesus ministered His healing love. She left a different person. The next night she and all of her children came along with her husband to the service. A son accepted Jesus. Her grateful letter arrived some time later. She wrote:

"I just wanted you to know that I received a healing from the Lord that night and such inner peace. I felt as if a ton of bricks had been lifted off my soul."

And then in a later letter:

DON'T LOSE HOPE

"The healing and inner peace have not left. I thank God every day for this. I read my Bible every day now and I get so much out of it, whereas before, the words did not have meaning for me."

She added a "P.S." to her letter, saying that her son had been healed of asthma.

GOD WANTS US TO BE WELL

"Unless an individual is willing to face the fact that his mental attitude toward the circumstances, not the circumstances, causes the unhappiness and depression, he is in my opinion, incurable."*

Praise God! He wants to change our attitudes!

God wants us to be well. He can heal us instantly or gradually. He may use a time of teaching to draw us closer and closer to Him. However, He will not do for us what we are able to do for ourselves. Whatever the reason for depression; no matter how severe it is; no matter how long you have had it; you can be set free. And "if the Son sets you free, you will indeed be free—"(John 8:36).

Many people are carrying such a heavy burden that they struggle simply to survive. They are physically, emotionally, and spiritually exhausted. My prayer for you is that God will lighten your burden, and that He will fill you with renewed strength. I pray that you will feel His presence and that you will know God does care, for He will walk through the dark valleys of

---

*How to Win Over Depression by Tim LaHaye (Grand Rapids, Michigan: Zondervan, 1974), p. 192. Used by permission.

depression with you. "All who are oppressed may come to Him. He is a refuge for them in their times of trouble" (Ps. 9:9). "The Lord lifts the fallen and those bent beneath their loads" (Ps. 145:14).

Above all, praise and thank Him. You cannot praise God and continue to be depressed at the same time. I'm not talking about flippant, tongue-in-cheek rhetoric, but an attitude of abiding praise, love, and worship; of saying, "Lord, I don't understand what is going on. But even though it may be difficult, I am going to trust and praise you."

Praise God no matter what your circumstances are, no matter what your physical problem is. Praise God no matter what your kids are doing. Praise Him no matter what job situation you are in or what your finances are. Praise Him for making you just the way He did. Praise Him!

VI

YOU CAN COME OUT
OF THE VALLEY

Whatever valley you're going through, whether it be a valley of disease, grief, or depression, remember: You are not alone. God said, ". . . I will never, *never* fail you nor forsake you" (Heb. 13:5). If you feel completely isolated, keep saying over and over, "I can *never* be lost to your Spirit! I can *never* get away from my God! If I go up to heaven, you are there; if I go down to the place of the dead, you are there" (Ps. 139:7,8).

We don't always see or understand God's plans, but He is sovereign, and not one thing happens to us that is not (as someone has said) "Father-filtered." There are no coincidences, just "God-incidents." He will not leave us alone, ever. He loves us. He *is* concerned. He *does* care, and praise God, He provided a Comforter for us: the Holy Spirit. Jesus told his disciples, "I will ask the Father and He will give you another Comforter, *and He will never leave you*" (John 14:15,16; emphasis added).

Jesus said, ". . . Don't worry about *things* — food, drink, and clothes . . ." (Matt. 6:25). Then He shared how He feeds the birds of the air and clothes the lilies of the fields. ". . . Your heavenly Father already knows perfectly well that you need them, and he will give them to you if you give him first place in your life and live as he wants you to. So don't be anxious about tomorrow. God will take care of your tomorrow too. Live one day at a time" (Matt. 6:32–34).

When we are desperate, that is the time we must rely on God's promises. When we are ready to give up, we must remember that "The Lord lifts the fallen and those bent beneath their loads" (Ps. 145:14). When the storm of life is raging around us, that is the time to draw even closer to the Lord and to hide beneath the shadow of His wings until the storm is past (Ps. 57:1).

As a loving and concerned Father, God says to His children, "Come unto me, all ye that labor and are heavy laden, and I will give you rest" (Matt. 11:28 KJV). "He gives power to the tired and worn out, and strength to the weak" (Is. 40:29).

There is not one thing that we go through here on earth that Jesus didn't go through by the way of the cross. And it is comforting to know our troubles are not permanent. "These troubles and sufferings of ours . . . won't last very long. Yet this short time of distress will result in God's richest blessing upon us forever and ever! So we do not look at what we can see right now, the troubles all around us, but we look forward to the joys in heaven which we have not yet seen. The troubles will soon be over, but the joys to come will last forever" (2 Cor. 4:17,18).

In *When You Get to the End of Yourself,* W. T. Purkiser wrote,

> The grace of God is not intended to save us from trouble. It is intended to save us from defeat . . . God permits some things which He does not purpose. There is a secondary or permissive will of God as well as His

primary or directive will . . . We can never avoid trouble. It is part of life in a sin-cursed world. But whether we rise above trouble in victory or go down beneath it in defeat depends, not on the hardships life brings to us, but on the way we react to them . . .*

Recently, after a meeting, the Lord impressed me that He was going to heal someone with a chipped bone. Soon, a young mother came up saying, "I'm the one. I have a chipped tailbone. I was injured four years ago in an accident and I have been in pain ever since.

"My husband and I are planning to go to another country as missionaries," she continued. "In fact, we are due to leave in a few weeks. But if I don't get rid of this back pain, I don't think I can go. I just don't know how I can be a missionary's wife and helper; I'm so discouraged and depressed."

"Well, first of all, let's ask God to take away your pain," I said. We prayed, but the pain did not go away.

The Lord seemed to say to me, *It's unforgiveness. This is blocking the healing of her back.*

"You need prayer for inner healing for some emotional wounds. Tell me more about yourself," I said.

She told me how her mother had abandoned her when she was eight months old and how she grew up harboring hate and bitterness toward her mother. Another tragedy in her life was the recent death of a baby son whom she had prayed and prayed for. I sensed that deep in her spirit was anger towards God for allowing this.

She was in a deep valley. She had been filled with the

When You Get to the End of Yourself by W. T. Purkiser (Grand Rapids, Michigan: Baker Book House, 1970), pp. 25, 23, 25. Used by permission.

Spirit but had stopped praying in the Spirit. She felt inadequate to be a missionary and to minister to others in boldness. Her spiritual life was in a valley; her emotional life was in a valley; her physical life was in a valley.

I called her by name and as gently as I could I said, "You must forgive your mother for abandoning you and also forgive God for allowing your baby boy to die." She knew what had to be done and finally said, "I forgive."

Oh, glory! The precious healing ointment of the Holy Spirit, the cleansing power of Jesus, the resurrecting and transforming power of the Father flowed through her. She began to praise God again in the Spirit. There was victory, light, peace, and joy on her face.

"Now, where is the pain in your back?" I asked.

"It's gone! It's gone!" she exclaimed. "I can stand up straight for the first time in four years."

Praise the Lord! How glorious it was to witness His "heavenly sunshine" flood her face. She went on her way that day thankful for being healed, excited about being free to go to the mission field, and rejoicing that because she was led out of her valley, she could confidently and with God's power lead others out of their valley, too.

An anonymous poet, one whose words have blessed so many lives, wrote:

> My life is but the weaving
>   Between my God and me
> I only choose the colors
>   He weaveth steadily.

YOU CAN COME OUT OF THE VALLEY

Sometimes He weaveth sorrow
And I in foolish pride
Forget He sees the upper
And I the underside.

We were extremely blessed to hear Jerome Hines, the Metropolitan Opera star, in concert. His rich, bass voice thrilled our hearts, but equally thrilling was hearing him share his vibrant faith in Jesus Christ. He related the story of his son, who has Downs syndrome, and the joys and blessings that this "special" child has been to his family. They could have called the existence of this child a disaster, but to him, to his wife, and to his other sons, it is a blessing. God's Word says in Isaiah 45:7, ". . . I send good times and bad. . . ."

We all go through valleys. There are times when it is hard to see the sun, times when we do not feel God or His presence at all. This is when we just stand on what the Word says, whether we see, feel, or hear God at all, just as this anonymous poet wrote:

I believe in the sun
   even when it is not shining.
I believe in love
   even when I feel it not.
I believe in God
   even when He is silent.

We are taught not to rely on feelings but on God's Word or our faith. But when we *don't* feel God's presence, it hurts terribly. There are times when we feel dead.

My little white narcissus bloomed in early spring. All

winter it had been dormant; then, one day it burst forth in bud and bloomed to bring beauty, fragrance, and blessing to all those who came to our door. Our lives are similar to this flower. Do you feel as if you're in a dormant stage right now? Do you feel weighed down with burdens, depression, pain, grief?

Oh, have faith! New life *will* come. Don't despair. Don't give up. Reach out to God and praise Him and trust Him. Praise Him even in this nonproductive, dormant time of your life. David said, "Why be discouraged and sad? Hope in God! . . ." (Ps. 42:4,5). Our hope does lie in God, whatever our problem, whether it be physical, spiritual, or emotional.

There will come a day when even as the little bud bursts forth, we, too, will bloom with new life, freedom, health, joy, and peace.

Remember, "They that wait upon the LORD shall renew their strength; they shall mount up with wings as eagles; they shall run, and not be weary; and they shall walk, and not faint" (Is. 40:31 KJV). God said in Jeremiah 29:11-13, "For I know the plans I have for you . . . They are plans for good and not for evil, to give you a future and a hope. In those days when you pray, I will listen. You will find me when you seek me, if you look for me in earnest."

"And now just as you trusted Christ to save you, trust him, too, for each day's problems; live in vital union with him. Let your roots grow down into him and draw up nourishment from him. See that you go on growing in the Lord, and become strong and vigorous in the truth you were taught. Let your lives overflow with joy and thanksgiving for all he has done" (Col. 2:6,7).

God's Word tells us to "Always be joyful. Always

keep on praying. No matter what happens, always be thankful, for this is God's will for you who belong to Christ Jesus" (1 Thess. 5:16–18). We need to learn as Paul did, ". . . in whatsoever state I am, therewith to be content" (Phil. 4:11 KJV).

In the depth of his valley, David said, ". . . I will praise the Lord no matter what happens . . ." (Ps. 34:1). The way out of the valley is through praise. Take His hand and walk through and out of the valley with Jesus, praising all the way—even though tears may be rolling down your cheeks. Stand on one of God's most precious promises: "When you go through rivers of difficulty, you will not drown. When you walk through the fire of oppression, you will not be burned up—the flames will not consume you. For I am the Lord your God, your Savior . . ." (Is. 43:2,3).

God will walk through the valleys with us. In fact, He will even carry us, if need be. God is always with us, but sometimes we don't realize He is sharing every experience. We receive wholeness when we consciously allow God to go back with us to those dark valleys and carry us through the valleys of depression, disease, death, and defeat.

When God takes our hand and walks through these very painful experiences with us, we see them in a different perspective, with spiritual maturity, and they no longer have the power to terrorize us.

Can valley experiences be useful? Yes, they can teach us compassion, gentleness, and perseverance. And they can teach us how to reach out to fellow strugglers, to lend a hand, and to make the journey easier for someone else.

To contact the author about speaking engagements, books, and tapes, please write:

P.O. Box 19827
Houston, Texas 77024